HOME·SWEAT·HOME

Other *For Better or For Worse*® Collections

Retrospectives

With Andie Parton

A *For Better or For Worse*® Collection by Lynn Johnston

Andrews McMeel
Publishing, LLC

Kansas City

08 09 10 11 12 RR2 10 9 8 7 6 5 4 3 2 1

ISBN-13: 978-0-7407-7096-8
ISBN-10: 0-7407-7096-9

Library of Congress Control Number: 2007939154

www.andrewsmcmeel.com

www.FBorFW.com

——— ATTENTION: SCHOOLS AND BUSINESSES ———

Andrews McMeel books are available at quantity discounts with bulk purchase for educational, business, or sales promotional use. For information, please write to: Special Sales Department, Andrews McMeel Publishing, LLC, 4520 Main Street, Kansas City, Missouri 64111.

DAD! MOM DOESN'T WANT THE CAT ON THE KITCHEN COUNTER!

IF I PUT HER FOOD ON THE FLOOR, THE DOGS WILL EAT IT.

JUST EDDY WILL.

SO, FEED HIM FIRST, THEN PUT HIM DOWNSTAIRS. DIXIE WON'T TOUCH THE CAT'S FOOD.

I WONDER WHY!

HISSSs

HISS AND HERS!

DEAR PAUL, I'M GETTING LESSONS READY FOR THE SUPPLY TEACHER AGAIN. THIS TRIAL IS TAKING FOREVER, AND I'M AFRAID TO ASK FOR ANY MORE TIME OFF.

TICK-TAP TICKATA TAP

I SPEND MOST EVENINGS IN MY ROOM. IT'S NOT THAT I DON'T LOVE MY FAMILY, I JUST MISS HAVING MY OWN SPACE.

TICK TAP TICK

I HOPE YOU DON'T MIND MY LONG LETTERS. I MISS YOU — AND WHEN I WRITE, I FEEL AS THOUGH I'M TALKING TO YOU....

TICK-TAP TICKITA TAP TICK TAP TICK

FACE TO FACE.

KLAKKK

WHY IS SHIIMSA IN HER CAGE?
BECAUSE... SHE STEPS ON MY KEYBOARD WHILE I'M WORKING.

CAN I TAKE HER DOWNSTAIRS?
OK, BUT KEEP HER OFF THE KITCHEN COUNTER, OR MOM WILL THROW A FIT!

STRANGE... EVER SINCE I CAME INTO THE KITCHEN, I'VE HAD THE FEELING THAT I'M BEING "WATCHED."

RELAX. I'LL GET HER DOWN.

ALL IT TAKES IS SUPERIOR INTELLECT.

Row 1

MISS PATTERSON, IS THE MAN ACCUSED OF ASSAULTING YOU IN THIS COURTROOM?

YES, YOUR HONOR.

PLEASE IDENTIFY HIM.

IN YOUR OWN WORDS, TELL THE COURT EXACTLY WHAT OCCURRED BETWEEN YOU AND THE ACCUSED ON AUGUST 11TH, 2005.

I WANT TO BE ACCURATE. I WANT TO BE FAIR. I DON'T WANT TO SOUND AS THOUGH I HATE YOU, HOWARD....BUT.... I DO.

Row 2

AT FIRST, I THOUGHT HE WAS JOKING... BUT HE WASN'T.

COME ON— DON'T BE SO UNFRIENDLY!

I FOUGHT WITH HIM. I BEGGED HIM TO LET ME GO.

I SCREAMED FOR HELP. I THOUGHT NO ONE COULD HEAR ME. ALL THE OTHER EMPLOYEES WERE OUTSIDE.

HELP!

BUT ONE OF MY FRIENDS WAS THERE. HE PULLED HOWARD AWAY FROM ME AND PUSHED HIM TO THE GROUND.

OWW!

I'VE KNOWN ANTHONY SINCE GRADE SCHOOL. HE'S SO EASYGOING. .... I NEVER KNEW HE COULD FIGHT!

NEITHER DID I!

Row 3

HOW DID IT GO?

OK... IT WASN'T AS HARD AS I THOUGHT IT WOULD BE.

ANTHONY? ELIZABETH? I MUST REMIND YOU NOT TO DISCUSS ANY ASPECT OF THIS TRIAL WITH EACH OTHER OR ANY OTHER WITNESSES UNTIL IT'S COMPLETELY OVER.

I UNDERSTAND.

YES. I UNDERSTAND COMPLETELY.

MR. CAINE? YOU'RE NEXT, PLEASE.

AND... SOME THINGS I DON'T UNDERSTAND AT ALL.

DAD....THERE ARE MORE EFFECTIVE WAYS TO KEEP THE DOGS OFF THE COUCH!

I KNOW....

BUT THIS WAY, THEY KEEP IT WARM FOR ME.

MOM-YOU'RE NOT GOING TO STAY AND WATCH THE TRIAL?

YOUR DAD IS THERE. I THOUGHT YOU MIGHT LIKE SOME COMPANY.

THEY ASKED IF I HAD EVER ACTED SEDUCTIVELY TOWARDS HOWARD. HE TOLD THEM I HAD PROVOKED THE ATTACK.. HE SAID I WAS PROMISCUOUS!

JUST IMAGINE HIM AS A RAT IN A TRAP, HONEY.... TRYING TO FREE HIMSELF.

I CAN'T.

...I'D FEEL SORRY FOR A RAT.

ARE YOU ALRIGHT, ELIZABETH?

YES, THANKS, SYLVIA. I'M JUST WORRIED ABOUT MY FRIEND, ANTHONY.

HE'S DOING VERY WELL. THERE'S JUST GOING TO BE SOME CROSS-EXAMINATION GOING ON. THAT'S ALL.

SYLVIA IS MY VICTIM SUPPORT COUNSELLOR. SHE'S WONDERFUL. SHE'S BEEN WITH ME THROUGH THIS WHOLE THING.

I'M SO PROUD OF YOU, LIZ.

I'M PROUD OF ALL THE PEOPLE WHO ARE TESTIFYING AGAINST HOWARD. IT TAKES COURAGE TO FACE SOMEONE IN A COURT OF LAW!

I DIDN'T HAVE A LOT OF COURAGE WHEN I WENT IN THERE, MOM.

...ALL I HAD WAS THE TRUTH.

I WONDER WHY IT'S TAKING THEM SO LONG TO QUESTION ANTHONY.

HOWARD ATTACKED ME, THERE'S A WITNESS— HE'S GUILTY! IT SHOULD ALL BE SO SIMPLE! ....

I DON'T EVEN KNOW WHY IT HAPPENED IN THE FIRST PLACE!

WHY WOULD A GUY RISK EVERYTHING—HIS REPUTATION, HIS FAMILY, HIS FREEDOM—FOR A FEW SECONDS OF PERSONAL...

POWER?

PEOPLE HAVE BEEN ASKING THAT QUESTION SINCE THE DAWN OF MAN, ELIZABETH.

...AND WE'RE STILL IN THE DARK!

WELL, THAT DOES IT. I CAN'T UNPLUG THIS THING. WE HAVE TO CALL A PLUMBER.

MAYBE LOVEY SALTZMAN HAS A SNAKE?!

A SNAKE?!

IT'S A PLUMBING TOOL, MEREDITH.

WHOA! IT'S NINE O'CLOCK, I HAVE AN ARTICLE TO FINISH, EDITING TO DO, I'VE MISSED DINNER AND THE MICROWAVE'S BROKEN. ...WHAT ELSE CAN GO WRONG?!

DADDY?

I GOTTA GO!

THERE'S YER SOCKS OUTTA THE SYSTEM, FOLKS, BUT SOMETHIN' ELSE IS CLOGGIN' HER UP PRETTY GOOD.

WE'LL NEED TO GO DOWN INTO THE NEXT LEVEL SOMEHOW, AN' OPEN 'ER UP!

THESE OLD HOUSES ARE A NIGHTMARE WHEN IT COMES TO PIPES AN' WIRING. WHAT ARE YOUR DOWNSTAIRS NEIGHBOURS LIKE?

BAM! BAM! BAM!!

...A BAD DREAM!

PARTON'S PLUMBING

LOOK, MRS. SALTZMAN. THE KIDS UPSTAIRS HAVE CLOGGED OUR PLUMBING, SO IT'S OUR RIGHT TO COMPLAIN ABOUT IT!

RIGHT NOW, SOME GUY IS BUSTIN' A HOLE IN OUR BATHROOM WALL. IT'S AN INVASION OF PRIVACY!

SO, TAKE A WALK. THE WORK MUST BE DONE.

WE SHOULD PAY LESS, FOR PUTTING UP WITH THIS!

I SHOULD CHARGE MORE FOR PUTTING UP WITH YOU!!

FOLKS! I'VE DISCOVERED WHAT WAS CLOGGING UP YOUR SEWER SYSTEM!—ANYONE RECOGNIZE THIS?!

IT'S.... NED!!

PARTON'S PLUMBING

WEED? COME DOWN HERE FOR A MOMENT! — WE'VE FOUND **NED**!

YOU WHAT?!!

NED WAS STUCK IN THE PLUMBING BETWEEN OUR PLACE AND THE KELPFROTHS' —WE THOUGHT HE WAS GONE FOR-EVER!

I PUT HIM DOWN THE PO- DIDN'T I, DADDY!!

YOU KNOW WHAT THIS MEANS, PATTERSON...

THE NED MAN IS **MINE**! OUR COVETED UNIVERSITY MASCOT IS **MINE**!!

COME BACK HERE, YOU WEASEL!!

RATS. I THOUGHT I WON HIM WITH A FULL HOUSE, BUT I'VE LOST TO A ROYAL FLUSH.

AND... WHAT IS NED?

OH... JUST A LITTLE PLASTIC GUY WEED AN' I HAD WHEN WE WERE IN SCHOOL.

HE HUNG ON OUR APARTMENT WINDOW. HE WAS OUR MASCOT, OUR ANTI-HERO, ... OUR FUTILITY SYMBOL.

WHEN WE MOVED, WE ARGUED OVER WHO WOULD GET HIM. HE'S SORT OF GONE BACK AND FORTH SINCE THEN.

IT'S KIND OF STUPID, REALLY. HE'S NOT WORTH ANYTHING.

MRS. SALTZMAN?

YOUR BILL FOR GETTING "NED" OUT OF THE PLUMBING SYSTEM, COMES TO $432.86.

I GAVE MRS. SALTZMAN A CHEQUE TO COVER THE RE-PAIRS TO THE PLUMBING... AND, I'LL PAY FOR THE KELPFROTHS' BATHROOM WALL.

ROBIN, THIS IS NOT A TOY, OK? NEVER, NEVER PUT ANYTHING IN IT THAT'S NOT SUPPOSED TO BE THERE—UNDERSTAND?

PUT IT THIS WAY: NOTHING GOES IN THERE THAT HASN'T BEEN EATEN FIRST!

MEREDITH, FINISH YOUR HOT DOG.

..... I'M THINKING.

HELLO, PAUL? I'VE BEEN TRYING TO CALL YOU! WHAT'S HAPPENING WITH YOUR TRANSFER?

REALLY? JANUARY?!! CAN YOU COME HERE FOR CHRISTMAS?... THEN... I'LL SEE YOU BEFORE NEW YEAR'S!

I LOVE YOU. KISSES AND HUGS. UH-HUH, MORE KISSES (GIGGLE) MORE HUGS... AND MORE KISSES...

SMOOCHY-SMOOCHY!

WHAP!

AND MORE HUGS.

APRIL, YOU CANNOT LISTEN IN ON MY PERSONAL PHONE CALLS!

BUT YOUR DOOR WAS OPEN, ELIZABETH!

IF YOU WANT SO MUCH PRIVACY, YOU SHOULD CLOSE THE DOOR!

AND YOU SHOULD HAVE THE COURTESY TO GIVE ME SOME PRIVACY, EVEN IF THE DOOR IS OPEN!

PFBLLTTT

WELL, THAT WAS MATURE!

WELL THAT WAS MANURE!

DAD!!

I'M OFF DUTY! FIX IT YOURSELF!

I HAVE ORGANIZED THIS FAMILY MEETING SO THAT WE CAN OPENLY DISCUSS SOME SERIOUS CONCERNS IN REGARDS TO OUR LIVING ARRANGE-MENTS.

AS YOU KNOW, APRIL AND I ARE NOW SHAR-ING THE UPSTAIRS... WHICH HAS RESULTED IN A SERIES OF, LET ME SAY, MISUNDER-STANDINGS... AND A NUMBER OF PROB-LEMS NEED TO BE IRONED OUT.

SO, WHAT WOULD YOU LIKE FROM US?.... DISCIPLINE?!

NO! I WANT YOU TO ACT AS A SOUNDING BOARD!!

SORRY. YOU TWO ARE BOTH OLD ENOUGH TO WORK THIS OUT ON YOUR OWN.

WELL, THEY DID WHAT YOU WANTED, LIZ.... THEY SOUNDED BORED.

KNOW WHAT I'D LIKE FOR CHRISTMAS, DARLENE? —A TOOL KIT!!! EVERYONE GIVES ME BATH STUFF OR CLOTHING, BUT A GOOD TOOL KIT IS SOMETHING EVERY WOMAN CAN USE!

I DUNNO WHY, BUT THE GUY WHO JUST RAN OUTTA HERE PAID FOR YOUR LUNCH!

YOU CAN COME IN NOW, MRS. RICHARDS.

THANK YOU, DOCTOR.

WE'RE SEEING SIGNIFICANT PROGRESS IN JIM'S ABILITY TO USE HIS HANDS, HIS LEGS ARE STRONGER AND HE STILL HAS HIS SENSE OF HUMOR!

BUT...HE CAN'T TALK!

WE'RE WORKING ON THAT. HE CAN SAY "YES" AND "NO"—WHICH IS A GOOD START.

AND YOU CAN HELP BY ASKING QUESTIONS THAT REQUIRE JUST A "YES" OR "NO" ANSWER.

I'M ALREADY DOING THAT, AREN'T I, JIM?

YES.... AND.... NO.

THIS PRESCRIPTION WILL HELP WITH HIS DEPRESSION. HE CAN TAKE IT AT NIGHT, BEFORE BEDTIME.

ANOTHER PILL. HE HAS SO MANY NOW.

AND HE TAKES THEM AT THE SAME TIME EVERY DAY?

YES. EVERY DAY, AT THE SAME TIME.

IRIS, HOW ARE YOU COPING WITH ALL OF THIS?

IT'S NOT EASY BEING A CAREGIVER. ARE YOU OK?—TELL ME. HONESTLY.

SNIFF

CAN YOU GIVE ME A PRESCRIPTION FOR SOME HUGS?

YOU'RE RECOVERING, JIM. A STROKE ISN'T THE END OF THE EARTH ANYMORE.

HANDIVAN

WE CAN DO THIS, YOU AND I. WE CAN MAKE YOU WHOLE AGAIN. I BELIEVE THAT!.... DON'T YOU?

WHERE THERE'S LOVE.... THERE'S HOPE.

outdoor lights

WHAPPA BOMP! WHAPPA BOMP!
WHAK-FWAM! WHAKK-FWAM!
BOOMM-WHAKKA-BOOM!

BOOMP-WHAPPA, FOOM-FOOM
BOOMP-WHAKKA, FOOM-FOOM
BOOMP, BOMP, BOOM, BOMP
FOOM-FOOM-FOOM-WHAKA

WRAP MUSIC!

19

THE FIRE STARTED IN THE APARTMENT DOWNSTAIRS. MR. KELPFROTH WAS SMOKING IN BED....

HE'D TURNED OFF THE SMOKE ALARM SO THE LANDLADY WOULDN'T FIND OUT. BY THE TIME OUR ALARMS WENT OFF, THE FIRE WAS OUT OF CONTROL. I TOOK THE KIDS DOWN THE FIRE ESCAPE.

MICHAEL RAN UP TO THE ATTIC TO GET HIS BOOK. THE FIREMEN GOT HIM JUST IN TIME. HE HAD TO BE CHECKED FOR SMOKE INHALATION...

I PICKED HIM UP AT THE HOSPITAL...AND WE ALL CAME HERE.

SO EVERYONE'S SAFE AND SOUND.

YES!

MERRY CHRISTMAS!

THEY SAVED THE OUTSIDE OF THE PLACE, MIKE, BUT THE WATER AN' SMOKE DAMAGE IS WICKED.

OUR SIDE OF THE BUILDING IS OK, BUT EVERYTHING STINKS!

FEH! I SHOULD HAVE EVICTED THOSE PEOPLE! WHO NEEDS THIS?! WHO NEEDS THIS?!!!

AND...THE KELPFROTHS?

STILL IN THE HOSPITAL, IN SERIOUS CONDITION.

HMPH!

FROM SMOKING, HE CAN KILL HIMSELF SLOWLY... IT'S HIS BUSINESS...BUT THAT SCHLEMIEL TRIED TO KILL US ALL!!

MAN, IT HAPPENED SO FAST. MY FAMILY WAS SLEEPING – AND THEN SUDDENLY, WE WERE ALL OUTSIDE!

WE DIDN'T KNOW WHAT WAS GOING ON UNTIL THE FIRE TRUCKS ARRIVED! THOSE GUYS CAME JUST MINUTES AFTER I CALLED!

I WENT UP TO THE ATTIC... BY THE TIME I CAME DOWN, I COULD HARDLY BREATHE...AND I COULDN'T SEE. TWO GUYS PULLED ME OUT... I WAS NEVER SO GLAD TO SEE SOMEONE IN MY LIFE!

WHAT?!!

YOU WENT UP TO THE ATTIC WHEN THE PLACE WAS FULL OF SMOKE?

I HAD TO GET MY LAPTOP, WEED – AND MY BOOK!

WELL, FOR YOUR SAKE, MIKE... I HOPE IT SELLS LIKE A HOUSE ON FIRE!

SO, WHAT ARE YOU GONNA DO?

FOR NOW, WE'RE GOING TO STAY WITH MY PARENTS. WE DON'T HAVE A LOT OF CHOICE!

CARLEEN AND I WILL BUNK IN AT THE STUDIO, AND THE SALTZMANS ARE STAYING WITH FRIENDS UNTIL OUR APARTMENTS ARE CLEANED. HEAVEN ONLY KNOWS HOW LONG THAT WILL TAKE!

MAN.... I FEEL SORTA ...SICK!

YOU'RE IN SHOCK, MIKE. YOUR WHOLE FAMILY IS. LOSING YOUR HOME IS A MAJOR TRAUMA. IT'S GOING TO TAKE A LONG TIME TO RE-COVER.

THIS IS THE KIND OF THING THAT YOU READ IN THE PAPER.... BUT IT'S ALWAYS HAPPENING TO SOMEONE ELSE.

WE'RE FINE, MOM. WE ARE STAYING WITH JOHN AND ELLY. NO, WE DON'T KNOW FOR HOW LONG.

WE'RE IN APRIL'S ROOM, APRIL HAS MOVED TO THE REC ROOM AND OUR KIDS ARE IN THE SEWING ROOM, NEXT TO ELIZABETH. WE'RE FINE!

YES, WE'VE HAD SOME FUN REORGANIZING AND IT'S A LITTLE CROWDED, BUT DON'T WORRY, EVERYTHING'S FINE.

EVERYTHING'S FINE. EVERYTHING'S FINE.

CLICK

FOR MY CHILDRENS' SAKE ..... EVERYTHING'S FINE.

WHAT ARE YOU THINKING ABOUT?

HOW IT ALL WAS BEFORE THE FIRE.

I CAN SEE THE CLOTHES IN THE CLOSETS, WHERE EVERY-THING WAS IN THE KITCHEN, THE KIDS' ROOM, THE HALL CARPET, THE PICTURES ON THE WALLS....

IT'S LIKE IT NEVER HAPPENED. WE'LL WAKE UP IN THE MORNING AND GO HOME.

WE'LL HAVE A PLACE OF OUR OWN AGAIN, DEANNA.

BUT, FOR NOW, AS LONG AS WE'RE TOGETHER.... WE'RE HOME.

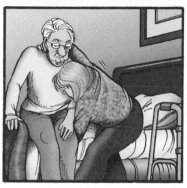

LET ME HELP YOU TO SIT DOWN, JIM. JUST THE WAY THEY TAUGHT US.

THIS IS LIKE DANCING, ISN'T IT.

THE TWO OF US MOVING TOGETHER AS ONE...

DO YOU KNOW THAT TONIGHT IS NEW YEAR'S EVE? ...WE'VE MADE IT THROUGH ANOTHER YEAR, YOU AND I.

ALRIGHT...

...LET'S DANCE.

DINGGGGG DONGGGG

I'LL GET IT!!!

HI!

HELLO, I'M FROM THE FIRE DEPARTMENT. IS DEANNA PATTERSON HERE?

NO, SHE ISN'T.

CAN I GIVE HER A MESSAGE?

YOU CAN GIVE HER THESE. THEY WERE LEFT ON THE FIRE ESCAPE. TELL HER WE WASHED THE BEDSPREAD AND CLEANED UP THE PHOTO ALBUMS.

YOU DID? WOW!

WE'RE NOT JUST FIREFIGHTERS, MISS... WE'RE FAMILY GUYS, TOO.

SHE'LL WANT TO THANK YOU!

JUST TELL HER TO HAVE A SAFE AND HAPPY NEW YEAR!

WHO WAS AT THE DOOR?

ONE OF THE FIREMEN WHO HELPED MIKE AN' DEANNA ESCAPE FROM THEIR APARTMENT.

HE BROUGHT THESE.

THIS ISN'T ALL THEY HAVE LEFT, IS IT?

NO, THERE'S MORE.

MOM SAYS THERE'S AN INSURANCE THING WHERE A CLEANING COMPANY GOES IN AFTER A FIRE AND SALVAGES ANYTHING THAT'S STILL GOOD. SO.... THEY'LL GET BACK SOME KITCHEN STUFF AND ANYTHING THAT'S NOT TOTALLY SMOKE DAMAGED.

COOL!

PERSONALLY, I'D RATHER GET ALL NEW STUFF!

YOU CAN'T REPLACE HISTORY, APRIL. EVERYTHING YOU OWN HAS HISTORY!

MAYBE **YOUR** STUFF HAS ......I'M NOT **OLD** ENOUGH TO HAVE "HISTORY."

DINNGGGGG DONGGGG

I'LL GET IT!

HEY, IF IT'S ANOTHER FIREMAN, ASK HIM IN. THAT OTHER GUY WAS HOT!!

WHOA! A HOT FIREMAN!!! — TOO FUNNY! — LIZ! IF IT'S **ANY** HOT GUY — LET HIM IN!

WARREN?!!

WHOA! SHE'S STILL AS PRETTY AS EVER!

WARREN—IT'S BEEN A WHILE! PLEASE COME IN.

THANKS.

HOOO! YOU'RE THE PILOT! YOU USED TO DATE MY SIS!!

APRIL...GET LOST.

I DON'T HAVE MUCH TIME, LIZ, SO I CAN'T STAY.—I KNOW THIS IS A CRAZY SUGGESTION, BUT I HAVE TO FLY NORTH, TOMORROW AND I COULD DROP YOU OFF IN MTIGWAKI IF YOU WANT TO VISIT!

WARREN, I HAVE MY TICKETS ALREADY. IF I COME WITH YOU, I'D GET THERE A DAY EARLY!—I DON'T KNOW WHAT TO SAY!

DON'T BE A DOOFUS! FIRST YOU SAY "YES", AN' WHEN YOU GET THERE, YOU SAY, "SURPRISE!!"

I'VE BEEN WORKING FOR A MINING COMPANY, AND I'M TAKING SOME DUDE TO A MINE SITE NORTH OF MTIGWAKI. I THOUGHT YOU'D BE PLANNING TO GO UP THERE ANYWAY, SO....

HMM

IT'S A GREAT OPPORTUNITY, ISN'T IT. .....I COULD USE MY TICKETS AT A LATER DATE. IT WOULD BE NICE TO GET THERE EARLY....

WAIT A MINUTE. I KNOW YOU, WARREN. WHAT'S GOING ON?

NOTHING! WE'RE FRIENDS, RIGHT? WHEN WE STOPPED SEEING EACH OTHER, WE SAID WE'D BE FRIENDS!

SO, FOR OLD TIMES' SAKE—YOU'LL COME WITH ME?

SURE. FOR OLD TIMES' SAKE, I'LL COME WITH YOU.

AND...WE SURE HAD SOME GREAT OLD TIMES!

MAN, YOU GET TO FLY TO MTIGWAKI IN A HELICOPTER. YOU ARE SO LUCKY!!

I KNOW.

I WASN'T SURE I'D BE ABLE TO GO—BUT THEY REMANDED THE TRIAL UNTIL NEXT MONTH—SO, I CALLED EVERYONE AND THEY'RE EXPECTING ME TOMORROW ....BUT—I'LL ARRIVE AT NOON TODAY!

PAUL WON'T BE HAPPY ABOUT YOU FLYING WITH WARREN.

IF PAUL WRIGHT IS CONCERNED ABOUT WARREN, HE IS TOTALLY WRONG!

...RIGHT!

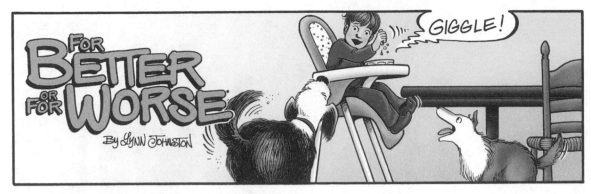

IS EVERYONE STRAPPED IN?

YES.

OK, HERE WE GO.

UH HUH.

YOU DON'T MIND SITTING UP FRONT, ELIZABETH? MY PASSENGER WANTED TO GET SOME WORK DONE.

ARE YOU KIDDING?!!

THIS IS THE MOST SPECTACULAR VIEW! —WOULDN'T IT BE GREAT TO BE AN EAGLE, WARREN?

SURE!

THAT'D BE COOL — IF YOU LIKE EATING MICE AND LAYING EGGS!

HEY! —I'M TALKING IN A ROMANTIC SENSE!

AND SHE SAID WE'D NEVER TALK ROMANCE AGAIN!

WE'RE HERE! I'LL CIRCLE 'ROUND THE TOWN. SOME-ONE WILL DRIVE UP TO THE AIRSTRIP TO GET YOU.

HERE'S A TRUCK ALREADY! IT'S GARY!

I'LL BE BACK FOR YOU IN 3 DAYS — HAVE FUN!

I WILL, WARREN. THANKS FOR THE RIDE!

GARY, IT'S SO GOOD TO SEE YOU!

HEY! I WONDERED WHO WAS BEING DROPPED OFF!

WHEN I SAW THE 'COPTER CIRCLING, I THOUGHT WE WERE GETTING A VISIT FROM SOME GOV-ERNMENT INSPECTOR!

WELL, IT'S ONLY ME!

WELL, GIRL —YOU'LL HAVE SOME IN-SPECTING TO DO!!

WE DIDN'T EXPECT YOU UNTIL TOMORROW, LIZ! —BUT VIV HAS THE GUEST ROOM MADE UP AND THERE'S A PIE IN THE OVEN!

SORRY TO BE EARLY, GARY —I JUST COULDN'T WAIT TO GET HERE!

THE FIRST THING I HAVE TO DO IS GET IN TOUCH WITH PAUL. HE SAID HE'D MEET ME AT THE BUS IN SPRUCE NARROWS. HE'LL BE SO SUR-PRISED TO KNOW THAT I'M ALREADY HERE!

YOU DON'T HAVE TO CALL HIM. HE'S IN TOWN. HE'S ...WITH SUSAN.

WITH SUSAN. WITH SUSAN?

WITH SUSAN AS IN "A FRIENDLY VISIT" OR WITH SUSAN AS IN, "WITH SUSAN?!!"

WELL...

I THINK YOU'LL HAVE TO WORK THAT OUT WITH THEM!

WITH PLEASURE.

KNOCK KNOCK KNOCK

COMING!

HELLO, SUSAN. PAUL'S CAR IS IN YOUR DRIVEWAY. CAN I SPEAK TO HIM, PLEASE?

YES! SURE!

ELIZABETH! I DIDN'T THINK YOU'D BE HERE UNTIL TOMORROW!

WELL... I GOT HERE A DAY EARLY.

AND I SEE IT'S ALREADY TOO LATE.

ELIZABETH! WAIT! I WAS GOING TO TELL YOU! I WAS GOING TO PICK YOU UP IN SPRUCE NARROWS AND....

AND WHAT?!! TELL ME YOU'VE DUMPED ME FOR THE TEACHER WHO TOOK MY PLACE?

I DIDN'T PLAN THIS... IT JUST HAPPENED!

LYING DOESN'T "JUST HAPPEN," PAUL! CHEATING AND PRETENDING AND COVERING UP DOESN'T "JUST HAPPEN"!!

BUT....

I DIDN'T WANT TO HURT YOU!!

WELL, GUESS WHAT!!

...IT JUST HAPPENED.

I HAD NO IDEA, VIVIAN. WE WROTE TO EACH OTHER, WE TALKED ON THE PHONE – I NEVER HAD A CLUE!

WHEN PAUL SAID HIS TRANSFER HAD COME THROUGH, I THOUGHT IT WAS TO TORONTO – BUT IT WAS TO SPRUCE NARROWS! ...HE WAS TRANSFERRED UP HERE!

HE'S A NORTHERNER, ELIZABETH. HE'D NEVER ADAPT TO THE CITY....., AND THIS THING WITH SUSAN, WELL, —ONE THING LEAD TO ANOTHER, AND....

YOU ALL KNEW I WAS COMING HERE. YOU ALL KNEW ABOUT THE TRANSFER. EVERYONE IN TOWN KNEW HE WAS DATING SUSAN. — WHY DIDN'T ANYONE TELL ME?!!

...WE THOUGHT IT WAS NONE OF OUR BUSINESS!

ELIZABETH, YOU'RE NOT ENTIRELY WITHOUT BLAME HERE. YOU LET PAUL THINK YOU WERE GOING TO STAY IN MTIGWAKI.

YOU ENCOURAGED HIM TO TRANSFER TO SPRUCE NARROWS—AND THEN, ALL OF A SUDDEN, YOU DECIDED TO LEAVE!....WHAT DID YOU EXPECT?!

—THAT A MAN WHO WAS BORN AND RAISED UP HERE WOULD FOLLOW YOU HOME?...HE WANTED TO! HE EVEN APPLIED FOR ANOTHER TRANSFER, BUT THE ORIGINAL APPLICATION WAS APPROVED FIRST.

HE'S A NATIVE MAN. SUSAN SHARES HIS CULTURE. WHAT HAPPENED WAS MEANT TO HAPPEN! YOU GUIDED THEIR JOURNEY.

THEN.....WHO'S GUIDING **MINE**?!

MARGARET! LOOK WHO'S HERE!

ELIZABETH! WE'VE BEEN EXPECTING YOU!

JESSE? OH, MY GOSH! YOU'VE CHANGED SO MUCH!

HE'S DOING GOOD IN SCHOOL, WHEN HE GOES—AN' HE LOVES MUSIC! HE PLAYS THAT HARMONICA YOU GAVE HIM ALL THE TIME!

HARMONICA?

SURE! THE ONE YOU GAVE HIM THE DAY YOU LEFT MTIGWAKI! CAN I MAKE YOU SOME TEA?

YES...THANKS.

HEY...HAVE YOU GOT A SECRET YOU WANNA SHARE?

NO...BUT I'VE GOT SOMETHING I WANT TO GIVE BACK.

WHERE'S ELIZABETH, MARG?

SHE'S HAVING A PRIVATE CHAT WITH JESSE.

THIS WAS MY GRANDFATHER'S HARMONICA.

I KNOW. I TOOK IT LAST YEAR WHEN YOU WERE PACKING. I WANTED SOMETHING OF YOURS...TO KEEP.

I'M SORRY, MISS PATTERSON. I SHOULD NEVER HAVE TAKEN IT.

NO, YOU SHOULDN'T HAVE. I SHOULD HAVE GIVEN IT TO YOU AS A GIFT.

HERE. LEARN TO PLAY IT REALLY WELL...AND REMEMBER ME, OK?

OK.

YOU TAUGHT ME A LOT. I WISH YOU HADN'T LEFT......I MISS YOU!

GIVE A GIFT, AND YOU GET ANOTHER IN RETURN.

WE'VE BEEN TO THE COMMUNITY CENTER, THE BAND HALL, THE NURSING STATION, THE COFFEE SHOP AND THE SCHOOL.

I GUESS I'VE SEEN EVERYONE I CAME TO SEE.

AND WHAT ABOUT PAUL. HAVE YOU NOTHING ELSE TO SAY TO HIM?

KNOCK, KNOCK, KNOCK, KNOCK.

COMING!

ELIZABETH, WE DON'T WANT TO FIGHT, OK?

I DIDN'T COME TO FIGHT. I CAME TO SAY GOOD-BYE.

AND PAUL...EVEN THOUGH IT DIDN'T WORK OUT FOR US, I WANT YOU TO KNOW THAT IF YOU EVER NEED A FRIEND....

THERE ARE SOME GREAT PEOPLE HERE IN MTIGWAKI.

I MUST SAY, GIRL—YOU DO TRAVEL IN STYLE!

I KNOW!

FLYING WITH WARREN SURE BEATS THE BUS!

WELL, THANKS FOR THE SMILES AND THE CHRISTMAS GIFTS YOU BROUGHT. TAKE CARE OF YOURSELF, AND KEEP IN TOUCH.

YOU TOO, GARY!

AND DON'T BE SAD FOR TOO LONG. HEARTS MEND, AND LOVE COMES AGAIN.

AND SOMETIMES...IT'S CLOSER THAN YOU THINK.

READY TO ROLL?

YES, SIR, CAPTAIN!

HOW WAS YOUR VISIT?

FINE.

YOU DON'T SOUND FINE.

REALLY. I'M FINE.

YOUR FRIEND PAUL IS WITH SUSAN DOKIS NOW.... THAT'S GOTTA HURT.

WARREN! YOU **KNEW**?!

WHEN YOU FLY IN THE NORTH, YOU HEAR THINGS. I DIDN'T THINK YOU'D BELIEVE ME IF I TOLD YOU.

SO.... YOU DROPPED ME RIGHT INTO THE MIDDLE OF IT !!!

I'VE NEVER DROPPED YOU, ELIZABETH.... I'M JUST HOPING WE CAN PICK UP WHERE WE LEFT OFF !!

FOR ONCE, I'M SIDING WITH YOU GUYS.

SHE'LL COME DOWN ON HER OWN, MOM.

SHE'LL CLIMB DOWN MY CURTAINS.

OH WELL.... WE NEED NEW CURTAINS ANYWAY.

WHOA! ... I CAN SEE ALL HER FILLINGS!

COME ON, SHIIMSA, LET'S FIND A LESS HOSTILE ENVIRONMENT.

MAN, THE REC ROOM IS A MESS. DEANNA'S MOM PILED A BUNCH OF STUFF IN HERE, THERE'S NO PLACE TO PUT MY CLOTHES OR MY HOMEWORK.....

Bedding linens

Towels

UNTIL MIKE FINDS A NEW APARTMENT, I'M CONDEMNED TO LIVE LIKE AN OUTCAST IN THE DUNGEON OF THE HOUSE. BUT I SHALL SURVIVE.

APRIL, YOU COULD TIDY UP A LITTLE! HOW CAN YOU STAND LIVING IN ALL THIS CLUTTER?

OH.

I'M SORRY I YELLED AT YOU, MOM.

WELL ... I HOLLERED AT YOU, TOO.

WE'RE ALL TENSE. WE'RE NOT USED TO SO MANY PEOPLE LIVING IN THIS HOUSE.

AND FOR SO LONG!

AT LEAST ELIZABETH'S GONE FOR A FEW DAYS. THAT'S ONE LESS IN LINE FOR THE SHOWER.

SLAM!

PAUL DUMPED ME FOR ANOTHER WOMAN!!

SPEAKING OF WATER WORKS...

WARREN KNEW PAUL WAS SEEING SUSAN! THAT'S WHY HE OFFERED TO FLY ME TO MTIGWAKI A DAY EARLY!

I THOUGHT IT WOULD BE A NICE SURPRISE—BUT IT WAS AWFUL, MOM! PAUL WAS AT SUSAN'S APARTMENT!

WHY DIDN'T HE TELL YOU HE WAS SEEING SOMEONE ELSE?

HE PLANNED TO...WHEN HE PICKED ME UP AT THE BUS. HE SAID HE WAS GOING TO BREAK IT TO ME GENTLY.

HONEY....

...THERE'S NO SUCH THING.

I AM SO MAD AT PAUL AND WARREN. I'M SO ANGRY, I COULD....

WHY ARE YOU MAD AT WARREN?

I THINK HE'S TOTALLY COOL! HE FLEW YOU UP TO MTIGWAKI, FOR ONE THING, AND HE EXPOSED YOU TO THE TRUTH!

I BET HE STILL LIKES YOU. WARREN STILL LIKES YOU! DID HE SAY HE STILL LIKED YOU?

APRIL-STAY OUT OF MY PRIVATE LIFE!

WHEN I'M RIGHT— I'M RIGHT!!

36

I THOUGHT THAT MOVING HOME WOULD BE A GOOD THING, BUT NOW I WISH I HADN'T.

I USED TO HAVE MY OWN APARTMENT, MY OWN STUFF. EVERYTHING AROUND ME WAS **MINE**!

NOW I HAVE NO BOYFRIEND, NO PRIVACY, NO IDENTITY...IT'S AS IF I'VE GONE BACK IN TIME...TO BEING A **KID** AGAIN!

HERE'S YOUR LAUNDRY, SWEETIE! DON'T FORGET TO PUT IT AWAY.

HOLY BOXES! WHAT'S ALL THIS?

EVERYTHING THAT WAS SALVAGED FROM OUR APARTMENT.

IT'S DISHES AND KITCHEN STUFF, MOSTLY. THEY'RE STILL WORKING ON THE FURNITURE.

WE'VE LOOKED ALL OVER OUR OLD NEIGHBOURHOOD FOR ANOTHER APARTMENT. THERE ARE A COUPLE OF POSSIBILITIES, BUT I DOUBT WE'LL FIND ANYTHING AS NICE.

WE'VE BEEN TOTALLY DISPOSSESSED!!

MOMMY?

WHEN ARE WE GOING HOME?

OH, I FORGOT TO TELL YOU, MIKE, A PACKAGE CAME FOR YOU TODAY...IT'S FROM SOME PUBLISHING COMPANY.

WELL...WHAT IS IT?!!

A CONTRACT! THEY'VE SENT ME A CONTRACT!

THEY'RE GONNA PUBLISH MY BOOK! - AND THEY'RE OFFERING ME A $25,000 ADVANCE!

WHOA!!

AYEEAA AHHHOO HAHAHAHAHA HAHAHAHAHA KHAHH OOOOO OOOOOO

IT'S TOO BAD OUR SON HAS NEVER BEEN ABLE TO EXPRESS HIS TRUE FEELINGS.

THEY'RE GONNA PUBLISH YOUR BOOK? WOW! THAT IS AWESOME!

MICHAEL, I'M SO PROUD OF YOU!

A $25,000 ADVANCE, AND RIGHT OF FIRST REFUSAL. THAT MEANS THEY WANT TO BE THE FIRST ONES TO SEE YOUR NEXT MANUSCRIPT!!

ISN'T THIS GREAT NEWS, ELIZABETH? SOMETHING BAD HAS TO BE FOLLOWED BY SOMETHING GOOD, RIGHT?

AFTER THE STORM BLOWS OVER, THE SKY BECOMES CLEAR AND BRIGHT!

WHAT'S THE MATTER?

...THE SUN'S IN MY EYES.

"DEAR MICHAEL PATTERSON. I OPENED YOUR PACKAGE, AND FROM THE FIRST PAGE OF YOUR MANUSCRIPT, I COULD NOT PUT IT DOWN."

"I RARELY SAY THINGS LIKE THIS, BUT YOU HAVE CRAFTED A SUPERBLY COMPELLING, INTENSELY EMOTIONAL STORY. WITH FEW ADJUSTMENTS, WE CAN INCLUDE YOUR BOOK IN OUR FALL LINE UP."

"PLEASE REVIEW THE ENCLOSED CONTRACT AND RETURN IT TO US WITH YOUR COMMENTS AT YOUR EARLIEST CONVENIENCE."

KNOW WHAT?

THIS IS REALLY HAPPENING!!!

YOU DID IT. AFTER ALL THOSE LATE NIGHTS OF WRITING AND REWRITING —YOU'RE THE AUTHOR OF A BOOK!

CONGRATULATIONS, MICHAEL.

WELL...THANKS FOR BEING SO SUPPORTIVE, DEANNA. YOU HELPED WITH EVERY PAGE!

—BY LEAVING YOU ALONE WHILE YOU WORKED?

NO....

...BY LOVING ME ALONE WHILE I WORKED.

SOMETIMES YOUR GRAND-FATHER SAYS AWFUL THINGS, MICHAEL. HE CAN'T HELP IT. HE TRIES TO SPEAK- AND SWEAR WORDS COME OUT!

WEIRD!

IT'S A CURIOUS PART OF HIS DISABILITY. ...WE'RE DEALING WITH IT.

THEY'VE OFFERED ME AN ADVANCE, IRIS! THEY SAY I'VE WRITTEN A BEST SELLER!

THAT'S LOVELY, DEAR!

✱@☆!! BOXCAR!! NO! NO! NO! NO! **NO!!**

HE WANTS TO BE INCLUDED IN THE CONVERSATION. HE WANTS TO HEAR MORE ABOUT YOUR CONTRACT.

HOW DO YOU KNOW?

I CAN READ HIM LIKE A BOOK!

SORRY, GRANDPA-I'VE BEEN TALKING WAY TOO FAST!-IT'S JUST THAT I'M SO **PUMPED!**

UH!

YOU KNOW...PUMPED? LIKE, REALLY EX-CITED?

YES, DEAR. I'LL GET IT FOR YOU.

HE FINDS PICTURES USEFUL WHEN HE CAN'T EXPRESS HIMSELF.

WHAT'S THAT, JIM? ...HE'S POINTING TO A CAR...AND... A GAS STATION!

PICTURE GALLE

THANKS, GRANDPA. - I'M GLAD YOU'RE PUMPED TOO!!

MY GRANDSON IS HAVING HIS FIRST BOOK PUBLISHED.... AND I CAN'T EVEN SAY "CONGRATULA-TIONS."

I CAN'T EVEN WRITE IT DOWN. I'LL TRY WITH MY LEFT HAND...NOPE!

DO YOU WANT TO WRITE SOME-THING, JIM?

STARTS WITH A "C". COFFEE? COLD? YOU WANT A CUSHION?

NO, NO, NO, NO, **NO!**

I'M DOING MY BEST. IF YOU'RE TRYING TO UPSET ME.... CONGRATULATIONS!

YESSS!

THEY CALL THIS CONDITION "APHASIA" ...IT SHOULD BE CALLED "CONFUSE-YA"!

MAY I HELP YOU, SIR?

YES....

I'D LIKE TO GET A VALENTINE'S DAY GIFT FOR MY WIFE.

WHAT ABOUT YOUR MOTHER!?

YEAH. RIGHT... WE'RE LIVING WITH MY MOM RIGHT NOW..... AND I HAVE TWO SISTERS!

OH... AND A YOUNG DAUGHTER.

YOU'RE LOOKING FOR FIVE GIFTS!

THAT MEANS I'D BE LEAVING OUT MY SON AND MY FATHER.

AND YOUR WIFE'S PARENTS?

YOU'LL NEED GIFT TAGS WITH THESE!

REALLY? UM....OK.

HAPPY VALENTINE'S DAY!

MERRY CHRISTMAS!!

I'LL GET OUR INTELLECTUAL PROPERTY GUY TO CHECK OUT THIS CONTRACT, MIKE — BUT IT LOOKS PRETTY GOOD TO ME.

THANKS, WEED.

SO, YOU'VE DONE IT! YOU'RE AN AUTHOR! HOW DOES IT FEEL?

TIGHT, MAN. THE ADVANCE WON'T COME UNTIL NEXT MONTH.

AND IN THE MEANTIME, I'VE GOT BILLS TO PAY, GET MY FREELANCE DONE, COMMUTE 2 HOURS TO WORK AN' LIVE IN CHAOS AT MY FOLKS' PLACE.

MIKE! STOP AND ENJOY THE MOMENT! YOU GOTTA CELEBRATE, MAN! THIS CALLS FOR A PARTY!!!

PARTY!

WE CAN USE MY STUDIO! LOOK AT THE SPACE! INVITE EVERYBODY, MIKE... I MEAN EVERYONE! FAMILY, SCHOOL BUDDIES, GUYS FROM WORK! MAKE IT BIG!

B.Y.O.B., RIGHT? WE LINE UP A FOOD TROUGH, SCORE SOME SEATS, WIND UP THE TUNES AN' TA-DAAH!

YOU'D THROW A 'PARTY? HERE?

MAN, AFTER WHAT WE'VE BEEN THROUGH, WE BOTH NEED TO UNWIND!

YEAH.

...IT'S BEEN A TENSE TIME, HASN'T IT.

BUT THE BEST PART IS....

WE'RE TALKING **PAST** TENSE, MIKE! — THE FUTURE LOOKS WONDERFUL!!

WE WERE ALL THROWN FOR A LOOP WHEN THE FIRE HAPPENED. I MEAN — MOVING OUT OF OUR APARTMENTS, HAVING TO GET THE SMOKE OUT OF EVERYTHING...

BUT LISTEN TO THIS! LOVEY SALTZMAN WANTS TO SELL THE PLACE — AND CARLEEN AND I ARE GOING TO BUY IT!

YOU ARE?!

WE OWN THIS BUILDING — ALL THE SPACE IS RENTED OUT. I HAVE COLLATERAL — AND... MY DAD IS GONNA GIMME A LOAN!

I THOUGHT YOUR DAD WAS OUT OF THE PICTURE, WEED.

WHEN IT COMES TO MAKING MONEY, MIKE ... MY DAD IS TOTALLY IN FOCUS.

EXIT

MICHAEL! JOSEF! SO GOOD TO SEE YOU!!

MORRIE AND I ARE MOVING TO A CONDOMINIUM. WE SHOULD HAVE DONE IT YEARS AGO. —JO TOLD YOU HE'S BUYING THIS PLACE? IT'S A GOOD THING. I GAVE HIM A GOOD PRICE. HE'LL MAKE IT NICE AGAIN.

WE'RE GONNA GUT ALL 4 APARTMENTS, PUT IN NEW WIRING, NEW PLUMBING — REALLY DO A JOB ON 'ER!

IT'S A BIG INVESTMENT, BUT EVENTUALLY, THE TENANTS WILL PAY IT OFF.

THAT'S TRUE.

YOU'RE YOUNG. YOU'LL LIVE LONG ENOUGH.

THIS PARKING LOT IS FULL, BUDDY.

BUT... I HAVE SPACE NUMBER 12.

LOOK, I'M RENTING THAT SPACE FROM A GUY CALLED CHUCK HASKINS.

HE NEVER TOLD ME NOTHING.

NOT RESPONSIBLE for ANYTHING

THAT'S MY SPACE! I'M PAYING FOR IT!

SORRY. I'LL NEED SOMETHING ON PAPER.

50 BUCKS IS "SOMETHING ON PAPER"

HEY! MOVE THAT CAR OUTTA SPACE 12!!!

MAN! PARKING IS EXPENSIVE ON THIS STREET!

YOU'RE TELLING ME!

MIKE? WE'RE HAVING A MEETING — WOULD YOU JOIN US?

NOW? SURE, BARRY.

MIKE PATTERSON EDITOR

AS PUBLISHER OF "PORTRAIT," I'VE BEEN COGNIZANT OF THE BOTTOM LINE, AND DESPITE INDICATIONS OF REASONABLE GROWTH, I SEE ROOM FOR FURTHER "ECONOMIZING."

I WANT THIS PUBLICATION TO BE MORE PROFITABLE!

WILL YOU BE DOWNSIZING THE STAFF, MR. GLUTTSON?

NO....

YOU WILL.

YOU LOOK PALE, MICHAEL. IS EVERYTHING OK?

NO, FRANCINE. IT ISN'T.

MR. GLUTTSON WANTS TO DOWNSIZE AGAIN. HE TOLD ME TO ELIMINATE ONE OF THE HIGHER SALARIED POSITIONS.

YOU HAVE TO FIRE SOMEONE? BUT WHY? WE'RE DOING SO WELL! WE'RE TURNING A GOOD PROFIT—AND WE'RE A GREAT TEAM!

I KNOW.

SO, HOW ARE YOU GOING TO ELIMINATE ONE OF US?

I'M NOT.

I'M GOING TO RESIGN.

I CAN'T BELIEVE WHAT JUST HAPPENED... I TYPED UP MY RESIGNATION AS CHIEF EDITOR OF PORTRAIT MAGAZINE..... AND I HANDED IT IN.

I'M GIVING UP MY FULL-TIME JOB—AT A TIME WHEN WE NEED IT THE MOST !!

WE DON'T HAVE A PLACE OF OUR OWN TO LIVE IN, WE DON'T HAVE A PILE OF SAVINGS, ... WHAT IS DEANNA GOING TO SAY WHEN SHE FINDS OUT ?!!

GREAT!! YOU FINALLY DID IT!!

MIKE FINALLY DID WHAT?

HE LEFT HIS JOB AT PORTRAIT MAGAZINE! I'VE BEEN BEGGING HIM TO QUIT AND HE DID!

WHAT WILL YOU DO NOW?

FREELANCE—AND I HAVE AN OUTLINE DONE FOR A SECOND BOOK.

I'M GOING TO BE THE BREAD-WINNER FOR A WHILE! AND... IF YOU'RE WORKING AT HOME, WE WON'T HAVE TO LOOK FOR AN APARTMENT IN THE CITY!

YOU'RE REALLY OK WITH THIS? ...I'LL BE A "KEPT MAN"!

YES... AND WITH LESS TENSION IN YOUR LIFE—I'LL BE ABLE TO KEEP YOU FOR LONGER!

WHERE ARE MOM AND ELIZABETH? AT THE COURTHOUSE. HOWARD'S TRIAL IS FINALLY OVER.

THEY WENT WITH ANTHONY TO HEAR THE VERDICT. MAN, THE TRIAL SURE TOOK LONG ENOUGH!

AT THE COURTHOUSE

I SENTENCE YOU, HOWARD BUNT, TO PRISON FOR 2 YEARS LESS A DAY, TO BE SERVED BEGINNING TODAY. PAROLE IN THIS CASE IS NOT RECOMMENDED, AND YOU WILL BE REQUIRED TO UNDERGO PSYCHIATRIC TREATMENT FOR...

I THOUGHT HE'D GET A LONGER SENTENCE. ME TOO. THEY WERE LENIENT BECAUSE HE SHOWED REMORSE.

HOWARD CAN SHOW REMORSE... BUT I DOUBT THAT HE CAN FEEL IT.

THANKS FOR THE LIFT, ANTHONY. THANKS FOR... EVERYTHING. ANY TIME.

SO, IT'S OVER. MAYBE HOWARD DIDN'T GET WHAT HE DESERVED, BUT IT'S OVER. GUESS WHAT ELSE IS OVER!

MIKE QUIT HIS JOB AT PORTRAIT MAGAZINE! HE FINALLY TOLD 'EM TO "STUFF IT"!!

WAIT A MINUTE...LET ME SIT DOWN. TOO MUCH IS HAPPENING. I NEED TO DIGEST EVERYTHING SLOWLY AND CAREFULLY.

YOU'RE IN LUCK! I MADE A POT OF 3-BEAN CHILI!

WELL, MY SWEETHEART, NOW THAT HOWARD'S BEEN SENTENCED, YOU CAN GET ON WITH YOUR LIFE ....MOVE FORWARD!

OR...DO YOU HAVE TO GET OVER PAUL FIRST ?!! ....BUT NOW THERE'S WARREN! ....HE'S A NICE-LOOKING CHAP. WELL-SPOKEN... GOOD MANNERS,

CALLS YOU UP QUITE OFTEN, DOESN'T HE! AHHHH, BUT IF I WAS A GAMBLER, I'D PUT MY MONEY ON ANTHONY!

DAD!!! WOULD YOU STOP ALREADY?! I'M SORRY.... I DIDN'T MEAN TO BE IRRITATING!

MEN!!

KNOCK, KNOCK, KNOCK!

THANKS FOR THE MAGIC, APRIL.

....WHAT MAGIC?

TODAY, YOU MADE THE SUN SHINE.

SNIFF SNUFF SNIFFF

SNOOFAH SNURF SNUFF, SNIFF

SNIFFAH SNOOFF SNOOF **SNUFF** SNIFF WHUFFL SNERFF

SNOOFFF-SNERFA **SNIFF-SNUFFLSNF** WHUFFAH SNIFFAH **SNIFF, SNERF...**

≡TSK≡ WHY DO THEY HAVE TO SNIFF AT TOTALLY EVERY SINGLE THING WE GO BY? THAT'S HOW DOGS KEEP IN TOUCH WITH EACH OTHER, APRIL....

SNIFF SNOOF SNUFF SNIFF

...SMELL PHONE.

SOMETIMES, IT'S BETTER TO BE BARKING UP THE WRONG TREE.

FOOMP!

THERE'S THE LITTLE HOUSE YOU LIKE, POP!

UH HUH.

HEY, I JUST THOUGHT OF SOMETHING! MIKE AN' DEE SHOULD BUY IT! THEY'RE GONNA GET $25,000°° SOON—THEY COULD MOVE HERE AN' BE RIGHT DOWN THE STREET FROM US!!

WOooo HOooo!!! I'M SO TOTALLY SMART!! I SURPRISE MYSELF SOMETIMES WITH MY OWN BRILLIANCE!!!

WHAT?

50

WHAT DO YOU THINK? IT'S THE CUTEST LITTLE HOUSE AN' IT'S JUST DOWN THE STREET! YOU COULD BUY IT AN' WE COULD BE NEIGHBORS!

WE CAN'T AFFORD A HOUSE RIGHT NOW, APRIL.

WHAT ABOUT YOUR BOOK ADVANCE?

WE COULD HELP YOU WITH THE MORTGAGE, SON! – I'LL TELL YOU WHAT — WHY DON'T YOU TWO SLEEP ON IT.

I'VE JUST QUIT MY JOB, DEANNA. WE CAN'T BUY A HOUSE NOW!

WE HAVE YOUR AD-VANCE, OUR SAVINGS — AND MY JOB IS SECURE.

WE CAN'T LIVE WITH YOUR PARENTS AND KEEP LOOKING AT APARTMENTS! – A HOUSE IS A GOOD INVESTMENT!

IT'S SUCH...A RISK!

WE DON'T KNOW WHAT MR. STIBBS WILL BE ASKING, WE HAVEN'T EVEN BEEN INSIDE! HOW DO WE KNOW IF THAT HOUSE IS RIGHT FOR US?... BESIDES — IT'S ON 3 LOTS! WE'D BE PAYING A FORTUNE JUST FOR THE PROPERTY!!

WE COULD SELL SOME OF IT! – AT LEAST, LET'S CHECK IT OUT!

FINE. WE'LL CHECK IT OUT.

I HOPE WE HATE THE PLACE!

I HOPE WE LOVE IT!!

I CALLED GEORGE STIBBS, DEANNA. HE'LL HAVE HIS HOUSE READY TO SHOW YOU IN A WEEK.

A WEEK?

FIRST HE HAS TO GET ALL HIS PAPER WORK IN ORDER, TALK TO HIS LAWYER AND SO ON.

HE'S BEEN LIVING ALONE FOR SOME TIME. I SUSPECT THERE'S SOME TIDY-ING UP TO DO. ≥TSK≤ THAT WOULD BE A PRETTY NICE PLACE TO HAVE, ALRIGHT!

YES! I THINK WE COULD DO QUITE WELL IF WE JUST SEVERED THE PROPERTY!

SEVER THE PROPERTY!?

WHERE WOULD I PUT MY TRAINS?!!

51

BELIEVE ME, OUR HOUSE IS MAYHEM RIGHT NOW. THERE ARE TOO MANY PEOPLE! — I HAVE NO PERSONAL SPACE!

I CAN'T HAVE A BATH WITHOUT LITTLE KIDS BANGING ON THE DOOR. THEY'RE INTO ALL MY STUFF — THEY USE MY COMPUTER....

MY SIS GOT DUMPED BY HER BOYFRIEND AN' SHE'S TAKING IT OUT ON EVERYONE. MY BROTHER AND HIS WIFE HAVE TAKEN OVER **MY** ROOM — I'M LIVING LIKE A **REFUGEE!**

NO, YOU'RE NOT, MAN... BUT I FEEL YOUR PAIN.

DID YOU SEE THAT, EVA? BECKY JUST WALKED BY... AN' GAVE US "THE LOOK!"

YOU KNOW: THE "I'M-BETTER-THAN-YOU'LL-EVER-BE-NO-MATTER-HOW-HARD-YOU-TRY" KINDA LOOK.

AND SHE'S ALL BY HERSELF.

SO?

IT'S LONELY AT THE TOP!

I WONDER WHERE MY MOTHER IS. SHE WAS SUPPOSED TO MEET ME HERE.

THERE SHE IS !!!

ELLY!!

APRIL, YOU CALL YOUR MOTHER BY HER FIRST NAME?

YEAH. IT'S SOMETHING MY SISTER TAUGHT ME...

IF YOU YELL "MOM" IN HERE... EVERYONE TURNS AROUND!

YOU NEED A NEW WINTER JACKET, APRIL. TRY THIS ONE ON.

UM...I DON'T LIKE IT.

MOM, CAN WE GO SOMEWHERE ELSE? THIS PLACE IS TOO.... YOU KNOW....

PRACTICAL.

OK, SHOW ME WHAT YOU HAVE IN MIND.

NOW SHOW ME SOMETHING I'D BE WILLING TO PAY FOR.

MY LIFE IS, LIKE, TOTALLY CONTROLLED BY OTHER PEOPLE... WHAT I WEAR, WHAT I DO, WHERE I GO....

I WANT TO BE TREATED LIKE AN ADULT. I WANT THE FREEDOM TO CHOOSE...TO HAVE AN OPINION...TO MAKE A DECISION AND BE RESPECTED FOR THE DECISION I MAKE!!

I DON'T FEEL LIKE COOKING TONIGHT, HONEY...SHOULD WE GET PIZZA OR CHINESE FOOD?

I DUNNO.

MOM?—WHEN AM I GONNA GET MY BEDROOM BACK?

AS SOON AS MIKE AND DEANNA FIND A PLACE TO LIVE.

THEY COULD BUY MR. STIBBS' HOUSE.

HONEY... THAT'S AN ENORMOUS DECISION—AND BUYING A HOUSE TAKES TIME!

YOU HAVE TO NEGOTIATE, SIGN CONTRACTS, GET A LOAN—AND MR. STIBBS HAS TO MOVE OUT!

I'M GOING CRAZY DOWNSTAIRS!

SOMETHING'S GOTTA HAPPEN SOON, OR I'LL BE THE ONE WHO'S LEAVING!

...CAN I COME?

GOOD. NICE AND SHARP?

SCRITTT
SCRITTT
SCRITTT

ELLY? WHAT ARE YOU DOING?

SHAVING THE SHEETS.

WHAT?

SOMETIMES, WHEN THEY'RE OLD, THEY GET THESE FUZZY LITTLE BALLS ALL OVER THEM...SO, I SHAVE THEM OFF!

SOMETHING GOING ON IN HERE?

YOUR MOTHER IS SHAVING THE SHEETS.

SERIOUSLY?

WHY IS THERE A CROWD IN HERE?

MOM'S SHAVING THE SHEETS!

OH, FOR HEAVEN'S SAKE!!!

THIS IS MY BEDROOM, OK? AND IF I'M SHAVING SOMETHING THAT YOU THINK IS WEIRD...

AT LEAST LET ME DO IT IN PRIVATE!!!

55

APRIL, CAN I USE THE BATHROOM? I'VE GOTTA GO TO WORK!

USE THE ONE IN THE LAUNDRY ROOM!

DAD'S IN THERE! WHAT'S TAKING YOU SO LONG!

OK, I'M **OUT!!** —HAPPY?

AAAGH! IT'S ALL STEAMED UP!!

UH... I'LL DEAL WITH THE STEAM IN THE BATHROOM.

WHO ATE ALL THE GRANOLA?

I DUNNO. ....MIKE, PROBABLY.

THERE'S NO MORE MILK!

HAVE TOAST, FOR HEAVEN'S SAKE! DON'T BE SUCH A PICKY FACE!

WHAT DID YOU CALL ME?

OH, FORGET IT, APRIL. WE'RE BOTH IN A HURRY. WE'RE BOTH UPSET.

I'VE GOT TO GO TO WORK. YOU HAVE A BUS TO CATCH. LET'S JUST GET ON WITH...

LARD BUTT!

SHE WHO LAUGHS LAST, LAUGHS BEST.

SNIFF

HI.... APRIL! ... ARE YOU.... OK? .... YOU... DON'T.... LOOK... OK.

HEY, SHANNON.

MY SISTER AND I ARE TOTALLY NOT GETTING ALONG. SHE THINKS SHE'S SO GREAT! THIS MORNING, SHE CALLED ME "PICKY FACE"! LIKE I WAS, SOME KINDA... I DUNNO.

I MEAN, HOW WOULD **YOU** LIKE TO BE CALLED "PICKY FACE"?!!

UM... OK, I GUESS.

IT'S... BETTER... THAN BEING .... CALLED... RETARDED!

SHANNON- WHO CALLS YOU "RETARDED"?!!
JEREMY JONES... BIANCA... MIRIAM... AN' THAT GUY... OVER THERE.

THEY... CALL... EVERY... ONE IN... SPECIAL NEEDS" RE- TARDED."
I HATE THEM FOR THAT!
I DON'T.

THEY... JUST DON'T... UNDER- STAND. THEY JUST... DON'T... KNOW US!
THEY'RE IGNORANT AN' THEY'RE MEAN!

WELL... IT'S... NOT THEIR ... FAULT IF... THEY... WERE BORN... THAT WAY.

APRIL, WHEN... PEOPLE CALL... ME... "RE...TARDED,"... DOES THAT... MEAN... THAT... I'M... STUPID?
NO! NOT AT ALL.

HAVE YOU EVER CHECKED OUT THE SIGNS AT THE AIRPORT? WHEN AN AIR- PLANE IS GONNA BE LATE ARRIVING, THE SIGNS IN FRENCH ALL SAY, "EN RETARD."

"EN RETARD" MEANS IT'S ON ITS WAY, BUT IT'S NOT THERE YET.
SO... WHAT... THEY'RE SAY- ING... IS... "I'M... ON MY WAY ... BUT I'M... NOT THERE YET"?
EXACTLY!

KNOW WHAT'S FUNNY?
WHAT?
THE PEOPLE WHO CALL YOU "RETARDED" WILL PROBABLY NEVER GET THERE AT ALL!!!

THE BAND'S GETTING TO- GETHER AT MY PLACE ON SATURDAY, APRIL. YOU COMIN'?
YEAH, BUT I HAFTA BE HOME BY 6.

MY BROTHER'S FRIENDS ARE THROWING A PARTY IN HONOR OF HIS BOOK BEING PUBLISHED -AN' I'VE GOTTA STAY HOME WITH THE KIDS.
WHOA! -YOU'RE NOT INVITED?!

YEAH, I WAS-BUT IT'S ALL OLDER PEOPLE, SO I MIGHT AS WELL MAKE SOME GREEN.
YOU'RE GONNA BE HOME ALONE? HEY... AFTER THE KIDDIES FALL ASLEEP, WE COULD PRACTICE!
PRACTICE WHAT?

WE'LL BE LEAVING NOW, IRIS.

IT'S BEEN A NICE VISIT, DEAR.

GOODBYE, DAD. TAKE CARE OF YOURSELF.

YES.

YES.

SEE YOU SOON.

JOHN, I WONDER WHAT'S GOING TO HAPPEN TO US. I WONDER WHICH ONE OF US WILL BE DEPENDENT FIRST.

...I THINK ABOUT THAT, TOO.

I WORRY ABOUT LOSING MY MEMORY.

I CAN'T IMAGINE WHAT WOULD HAPPEN IF I COULDN'T RE-MEMBER WHO YOU WERE!

WELL.....

WE'D JUST HAVE TO KEEP FALLING IN LOVE OVER AND OVER AGAIN.

WHO ARE YOU TAKING TO MIKE'S PARTY? I ASKED WARREN, BUT IT'S NOTHING SERIOUS. IT'S JUST "A DATE."

REALLY—IF HE'S "JUST A DATE," WHY ARE YOU GETTING ALL DRESSED UP?

NO POINT IN WEARING GRUBS!

IS HE GONNA FLY YOU TO WEED'S PLACE? NO.

HE HAS A CAR. I TOLD YOU, IT'S NOTHING SPECIAL. I JUST WANTED SOMEONE TO KEEP ME COMPANY.

IF YOU'RE WEARING THAT, YOU'LL WANT "SOMEONE" TO KEEP YOU WARM!

SHRIEK! CAN'T CATCH ME! CAN'T CATCH ME!

THE SECRET TO SUCCESSFUL BABY-SITTING IS TO WEAR THE KIDS OUT.

Congratulations Mike

I'M GLAD YOU COULD COME WITH ME TONIGHT, WARREN!

WHOA! THIS IS SUCH A COOL PLACE!

THESE ARE ALL MIKE'S FRIENDS. SOME OF THEM HE'S KNOWN SINCE GRADE SCHOOL. OTHERS ARE WRITERS AND ILLUSTRATORS, BUSINESS ASSOCIATES...

WHAT IS THIS—A PHOTO STUDIO? UH-HUH. JO HAS SHOT SOME OF THE BEST-KNOWN MODELS!

WHOA!—ASK HIM TO BAG A COUPLE FOR ME!!

60

LADIES AND GENTOIDS, MAY I HAVE YOUR ATTENTION, PLEASE!

TONIGHT'S SOIRÉE IS IN HONOR OF WRITER EXTRAORDINAIRE— MICHAEL PATTERSON! HE HAS JUST SIGNED HIS FIRST CONTRACT WITH A PUBLISHER...

ON BEHALF OF YOUR FRIENDS AND FAMILY— AND THIS IS FROM THE HEART, MAN..... CONGRATULATIONS ON BECOMING AN **AUTHOR!**

MIKE! MIKE! MIKE

MIKE! MIKE!

UM....I...DON'T KNOW WHAT TO SAY.

OH, JOHN (SNIFF!) I'M SO PROUD! I'VE BEEN READING MICHAEL'S WORK, HELPING TO EDIT...I ALWAYS HOPED HE'D FIND A PUBLISHER...AND NOW... HONK

THIS IS PRETTY AMAZING, LIZ!

YES.— I FEEL KIND OF INSIGNIFICANT NEXT TO MY FAMOUS BROTHER!

WELL, HE'S NOT FAMOUS YET, BUT....

HEY. YOU'LL NEVER BE INSIGNIFICANT!

NO?

YOU COULD BECOME MY "SIGNIFICANT" OTHER!

ELIZABETH! INTRODUCE US TO YOUR FRIEND!

GORDON AND TRACEY MAYES, THIS IS WARREN BLACKWOOD.

WHOA! YOU OWN MAYES MOTORS OUT ON THE HIGHWAY, RIGHT?!!

IT LOOKS LIKE GORDON AND WARREN HAVE HIT IT OFF! ....IS HE YOUR NEW BEAU?

I DON'T WANT A NEW BEAU, TRACEY.

....THE LAST ONE LEFT TOO MANY ARROWS.

GERALD! WHAT ARE YOU DOING HERE?

ARE THE KIDS ASLEEP?

YEAH, BUT...

LOOK, I BROUGHT A BOTTLE OF WINE AN' SOME TUNES! WE'RE GONNA HAVE OUR OWN PARTY!

HOW DID YOU GET HERE?

I BUMMED A RIDE! MY FOLKS THINK I'M OUT WITH THE GUYS. I HAVE UNTIL 12:30. GOT ANY FOOD?

THIS REC ROOM IS PERFECT, APRIL! WE HAVE EVERYTHING!

YEAH—A BOOM BOX, GAME STATION, BIG TV....

AND...COMFY ACCOMMODATION!

IT'S KIND OF CROWDED IN HERE, HONEY—AND IT'S GETTING LATE. I THINK YOUR DAD AND I WILL BE HEADING HOME.

THANKS FOR COMING, MOM!

MIKE HAS SOME WONDERFUL FRIENDS!

YES—THAT WAS QUITE THE PARTY!...I'M AFRAID I CAN'T TAKE TOO MUCH OF THAT SORT OF THING ANYMORE.

I HOPE APRIL ISN'T HURT THAT WE WENT WITHOUT HER.

SHE WAS INVITED, ELLY. SHE SAID SHE'D RATHER STAY HOME AND BABY-SIT!

BESIDES, SHE WOULD HAVE HAD A LOT MORE FUN IF SHE WAS WITH PEOPLE HER OWN AGE.

GRRAAAAAKKKKKK

WHAT WAS THAT?

I DUNNO...SOUNDS LIKE THE GARAGE DOOR OPENING!

MY PARENTS ARE HOME!

BUT, IT'S ONLY 11 O'CLOCK!

GET YOUR COAT ON! HURRY! YOU GOTTA GO!!!

BACK DOOR! BACK DOOR!—I'LL CALL A CAB!

I DON'T HAVE ANY MONEY!

HI, HONEY! WE THOUGHT WE'D FIND YOU IN BED!

I WAS!

...BUT I'M NOT....AND YOU DIDN'T!

HOW WERE THE LITTLE ONES? DID THEY GO TO BED OK?
UH-HUH. THEY WERE FINE.

DID YOU HAVE A NICE EVENING?
I JUST WATCHED T.V.

WHAT DID YOU WATCH? A MOVIE?
REALITY SHOW?
NAH, JUST STUFF.
NOT REALLY.

SO, NOTHING EXCITING TO TALK ABOUT.
NOPE.

THANK GOODNESS!!!
Oooooo

SEE YOU IN THE MORNING, HONEY. THANKS FOR HOLDING DOWN THE FORT.
G'NIGHT, DAD.

MONEY! GOTTA FIND SOME MONEY!
HELLO? COULD YOU SEND A CAB TO SHARON PARK DRIVE?

GERALD! DITCH THE BOTTLE! HERE'S 14 BUCKS. IT'S ALL I'VE GOT. A CAB'S GONNA MEET YOU ON THE CORNER!

GO!

SIGH ···· IT'S SO NICE TO KNOW WE HAVE A TEENAGER WE DON'T HAVE TO WORRY ABOUT!

THAT WAS A FUN PARTY, LIZ. I'M GLAD YOU INVITED ME.
I AM TOO. I HAD A NICE TIME.

WE'RE GOING TO GET TOGETHER AGAIN... AREN'T WE?
I LIKE YOU, WARREN. I REALLY DO. LET'S JUST SEE WHAT HAPPENS.... OK?

I'LL BE FLYING OUT TOMORROW BUT I'LL BE BACK IN A WEEK. I'LL SEE YOU THEN. TELL ME YOU'LL SEE ME IN A WEEK! I'M NOT LEAVING UNTIL YOU SAY YOU'LL SEE ME!
SAY YES!
YES.

I'M NOT GONNA WAIT TILL TOMORROW... I'M FLYING NOW!!!

For **Better** or For **Worse**
By Lynn Johnston

IT'S MAH BIRTHDAY, AN' IM SAYIN' IT **LOUD,** IT'S MAH BIRTHDAY, AN' AH GOTTA BE **PROUD.** I'M 16, I'M NOT A KID ANYMORE, I'M GONNA BE DRIVING WITH MY FOOT TO THE FLOOR.

GOTTA SHOW THE WORLD THAT I'M IN CHARGE OF MAH STUFF— I'M A WOMAN! I'M A WOMAN—AN' I'M STRONG AN' I'M TOUGH, SO WATCH ME, BABY—COMIN' OUTTA MY SHELL, **YEAH!** WATCH ME, BABY, GONNA RAISE A LITTLE....

HELL...O, MOM!

YOUR CAKE IS READY.

HAPPY BIRTHDAY, APRIL!

SHE'S 16 AN' SHE'S **SMOKIN'**!!

I MEAN THAT IN AN ALLEGORICAL SENSE, SIR.

CUT UP YOUR CAKE, GIRL—AN' LET'S PARTY!

THANKS FOR THE GIFTS, EVERYONE!

THE CAKE WAS GREAT, MOM. WE'LL BE BACK BY ONE A.M.

HAVE FUN, HONEY.

THERE SHE GOES. IT SEEMS LIKE YESTERDAY SHE WAS JUST A BABY.

NOW, SHE'S A LOVELY YOUNG WOMAN.

OUR CHILDREN HAVE ALL GROWN UP, ELLY.

ARE YOU THINKING WHAT I'M THINKING?

WE DID IT!

Lynn

 FFFFTTTT

 GOOD MORNING, BABY SIS!

 WHAT THE HECK IS THAT?!! APRIL AT 16.

 WAS THAT APRIL? THAT'S OUR YOUNGEST DAUGHTER AT THE AGE OF 16, ELLY.

 EVERYTHING'S GOING TO BE CHANGING NOW. —SHE'S DRIVING AGE. YEAH.

 ...SHE'S GOING TO BE DRIVING US CRAZY!

 WHOA! CONGRATULATIONS ON THE BIRTHDAY, APRIL! SWEET 16 AN' "NEVER BEEN KISSED"!!!

 OH, I WOULDN'T SAY THAT! SHUT UP, GERALD! HOOOO!

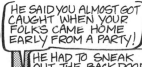 HE SAID YOU ALMOST GOT CAUGHT WHEN YOUR FOLKS CAME HOME EARLY FROM A PARTY! HE HAD TO SNEAK OUT THE BACK DOOR AN' GRAB A TAXI!

 WHY ARE YOU TELLING THE GUYS ABOUT THINGS THAT ARE TOTALLY PERSONAL? HEY, YOU'VE TOLD YOUR GIRL-FRIENDS, HAVEN'T YOU?

 THAT'S DIFFERENT. TO US, IT'S A SECRET... TO YOU, IT'S A SCORE!!

CAN I TALK TO YOU, LIZ?

YEAH. SURE. I'M JUST LOOKING FOR AN APARTMENT.

THIS PLACE IS TOO CROWDED. I CAN'T GET ANYTHING DONE. NOBODY HAS ANY PRIVACY.

MIKE AND DEANNA STILL HAVEN'T DECIDED WHAT TO DO, SO I'M MAKING A DECISION. I'M MOVING OUT.

I WANT MY OWN PLACE ANYWAY. LIVING AT HOME CRAMPS MY STYLE.

YOU HAVE A STYLE?!

DO YOU WANT SOME CRAMPS?!

I JUST SAW ELIZABETH DRIVE AWAY, APRIL. — DO YOU KNOW WHERE SHE'S GOING?

TO CHECK OUT AN APARTMENT.

IF ELIZABETH FINDS A NICE APARTMENT, YOU CAN MOVE BACK UPSTAIRS!

I DON'T WANT HER ROOM, MOM— I WANT MY OWN ROOM BACK!

WELL, I'M SURE MIKE AND DEANNA WILL FIND SOMETHING SOON. THEY'RE THINKING ABOUT BUYING A HOUSE.

MR. STIBBS' HOUSE?

SPLORP!

I DOUBT IT. THERE ARE ONLY 2 BEDROOMS AND THE PROPERTY'S A PROBLEM. IT'S FAR TOO BIG. THEY'D HAVE TO SEVER THE LAND, ADD ON TO THE HOUSE...

BUT WE'RE GOING TO LOOK AT IT ANYWAY.

WHY?

I'VE NEVER BEEN INSIDE MR. STIBBS' HOUSE!

SO, WITH WHAT YOU HAVE IN THE BANK, PLUS THE MONEY DEE'S PARENTS HAVE OFFERED YOU — THE ADVANCE ON YOUR BOOK, AND SOME HELP FROM US...

— I THINK YOU COULD EASILY AFFORD TO BUY A HOUSE IN THIS NEIGHBORHOOD.

DON'T LOOK SO WORRIED! WE'VE DONE THE MATH!

BESIDES, THE COST OF RENTING AN APARTMENT, EVEN THIS CLOSE TO TORONTO, WOULD...

I KNOW, I KNOW.

IT'S JUST THAT BUYING A HOUSE IS SUCH A HUGE DECISION. IT'S A LIFE-CHANGING COMMITMENT.... IT'S...

... ALMOST AS BAD AS GETTING MARRIED!!

DADDY? YES, MEREDITH!

...WHEN DO THEY GET TO THE PART WHERE JESUS MEETS THE EASTER BUNNY?

HEY THERE, GEORGE!

HI, JOHN!... TAKING THE DAY OFF?

YEAH. I DECIDED TO DO THE SPRING CLEAN-UP, FIX THE BACK DOOR, RAKE THE YARD. YOU KNOW...ALL THE THINGS A GUY HATES DOING.

SO... YOU'RE WALKING THE DOGS.

YEAH. ANY EXCUSE TO PUT OFF WORK IS FINE WITH ME.

I JUST PUT A POT OF COFFEE ON.

FINE WITH ME!

I'VE HAD AN APPRAISAL DONE ON THIS PLACE, JOHN....

LOOKS LIKE IT'S WORTH QUITE A SUM—WITH THE PROPERTY AND ALL. DO YOU THINK YOU'D BE INTERESTED?

UMM... WHEN CAN WE COME AND LOOK IT OVER?

ANY TIME, NOW. I'VE CLEANED 'ER UP SOME. SHE'S IN PRETTY GOOD SHAPE. I HATE TO SELL, BUT I CAN'T LIVE HERE ALONE. NOPE. CAN'T DO IT.

MY BOYS TELL ME TO RE-MARRY...BUT WHEN LOIS DIED, I DECIDED THAT FROM THEN ON.... I'D GO IT ALONE.

I THINK.... IF ELLY DIED... I'D DO THE SAME THING.

YEP.

...ONCE IS ENOUGH.

WHAT A LOVELY HOUSE, GEORGE!

UH-HUH... WE DESIGNED IT FOR OUR RETIREMENT.

WEREN'T TOO MANY BUILDINGS HERE WHEN WE BOUGHT THE PROPERTY. NOW IT'S QUITE A COMMUNITY. WE ONLY HAD 10 YEARS HERE BEFORE LOIS DIED.

YOUR DAD HAS ALWAYS LOVED THIS CORNER LOT. WHAT DO YOU THINK, MICHAEL?

IT'S PRETTY NICE, ALRIGHT.

BUT THERE ARE ONLY 2 BEDROOMS.

YES, THE HOUSE IS SMALL.

BUT... YOU COULD ADD ON!!

DAD! FOR WHAT THIS HOUSE AND PROPERTY ARE WORTH...DEANNA AND I COULD BUY YOUR PLACE!!

THAT'S NOT A BAD IDEA, JOHN! YOU AND ELLY WOULD FIT IN HERE LIKE FINGERS IN A GLOVE!

YOU TALKED ABOUT SETTING YOUR TRAINS OUT BACK THERE ON THE PROPERTY—I'D SAY THE POTENTIAL HERE IS FOR YOU TWO... NOT THE KIDS!

SELL THEM **YOUR** PLACE!!

GEORGE'S SUGGESTION HAS MERIT, ELLY.

—WHY DON'T WE THINK ABOUT IT?

YOU MEAN, "WHY DON'T **I** THINK ABOUT IT?"

IT LOOKS LIKE YOU'VE ALREADY MADE UP YOUR MIND!

WELL, THAT WAS AN EXCITING VISIT, WASN'T IT! .... SELLING THIS HOUSE TO THE KIDS AND MOVING DOWN THE STREET MAKES SENSE!

WHY IS EVERYONE SO QUIET?

YOU'RE WAY AHEAD OF US, JOHN! BESIDES YOU AND I HAVE 30 YEARS OF STUFF IN THIS HOUSE!

YOU'RE ALSO FORCING MIKE AND DEANNA TO MAKE A HUGE DECISION!

IT COULD WORK, MOM....

... I'VE ALWAYS LOVED THIS HOUSE.

WAIT A MINUTE!

I LIVE HERE! .... WHAT ABOUT ME?!

IF YOU SELL THIS HOUSE TO MIKE AND DEANNA—WHERE WOULD **I** GO?!

THE STIBBS' HOUSE HAS 2 BEDROOMS, APRIL.

BUT I LIKE IT HERE! I'M NOT **READY** TO MOVE!!!

THEN, YOU CAN STAY HERE WITH **US!**

WE'D **LOVE IT** IF YOU STAYED WITH US! —WHY DON'T YOU STAY WITH US?!!

... I DON'T WANT TO BE A LIVE-IN BABY SITTER !!!

DON'T LOOK SO WORRIED, HONEY. NOTHING'S BEEN DECIDED YET. IT'S ALL "WHAT IF?"

WHAT IF?

WE'RE THINKING, THAT'S ALL! YOU KNOW: "WHAT IF YOUR MOM AND I MOVED TO A SMALLER PLACE DOWN THE STREET?"

WHAT IF MICHAEL AND DEANNA LIVED HERE? IT'S A PERFECT HOUSE FOR THEM AND TOO BIG FOR US!

....IT'S ALL JUST "WHAT IF."

I THINK "WHAT IF" IS GOING TO TURN INTO "WHAT IS"!!

GLOOM···GLOOM···GLOOM

I DID IT, APRIL! I FOUND AN APARTMENT!

HEY, ARE YOU LISTENING TO ME?

WHY? YOU NEVER LISTEN TO ME.

I CAN MOVE IN NEXT MONTH! YOU CAN MOVE UPSTAIRS AGAIN! YOU CAN HAVE **MY** ROOM!

ELIZABETH, MIKE AND DEANNA MIGHT BUY THIS HOUSE. IF THEY DO, I'LL HAVE TO DECIDE WHERE I WANT TO LIVE —HERE OR WITH MOM AN' DAD!

SO? WHERE DO YOU WANNA BE?

HOW BIG IS YOUR PLACE?!!

WHAT ARE YOU THINKING?

MY PARENTS' PLACE LOOKS DIFFERENT TODAY.

IF DAD CONVINCES MOM TO MOVE TO THE STIBBS' PLACE...

I'D LOVE TO LIVE HERE, MICHAEL!

MERRIE AND ROBIN CAN PLAY IN THE SAME PARK YOU PLAYED IN, SLIDE DOWN THE SAME RAVINE, MAKE FORTS IN THE SAME YARD, GO TO THE SAME SCHOOLS...

SIGH···...NOTHING'S GONNA BE THE SAME.

JOHN, IF WE MOVED TO A SMALLER HOUSE, WHAT WOULD WE DO WITH ALL OUR STUFF?

LEAVE IT HERE.

....LEAVE IT?...HERE?

MIKE AND DEANNA LOST ALMOST EVERYTHING IN THE FIRE! — WE LEAVE THEM OUR FURNITURE AND EVERYTHING IN THE CUPBOARDS AND GET **NEW** STUFF!!

NEW STUFF?

TOTALLY NEW!! NEW BED, NEW SHEETS, NEW TOWELS, NEW POTS AND PANS, NEW COUCH, NEW TV....

EVERYTHING NEW?!

EXCEPT ME. I'D STAY THE SAME.

Lynn

HI, WARREN! GOT AN APT NTNG SPCL, 1 RM, BSMT OLD HSE, BT CLS TO WRK. CNT WT TO BE ON MY OWN AGN.

MY FLKS PLC IS CRZY. HW R U? WHN WL U B BK N TWN? HP U R....

OW!

GOT A CASE OF T.M.D.I.?

YEAH. SERIOUS.

"TEXT MESSAGE DIGITAL INJURY" IS GOING TO BE THE NEXT BIG HEALTH ISSUE!

Lynn

I'M GLAD YOU FOUND AN APARTMENT, LIZ!

YEAH. ....LOOKS LIKE OUR WHOLE FAMILY IS GOING TO BE UP-ROOTED.

WHY DO YOU SAY THAT?

YOU'RE GOING TO BUY THE STIBBS' PLACE, RIGHT? MIKE AND DEANNA ARE GOING TO STAY HERE.

WELL, IT HASN'T BEEN DECIDED YET.

YES IT HAS!!

YOU'RE LOOKING AT FURNITURE CATALOGUES, MIKE AN' DEE ARE DOWN AT THE BANK, AND DAD'S CLEANING OUT HIS WORKSHOP!

SO, I'D SAY IT'S BEEN DECIDED.

OH.

Lynn

72

FOR **BETTER** OR FOR **WORSE**

By Lynn Johnston

THIS AFTERNOON, WE'RE GOING TO GO OVER SOME ENGLISH GRAMMAR.

GROANNN!!

BUT WE DONE THAT LAST WEEK!

FACT: NO MATTER HOW CAPABLE, NO MATTER HOW INTELLIGENT YOU ARE — POOR GRAMMAR WILL MAKE YOU SOUND LESS INTELLIGENT AND POORLY EDUCATED. SO LET'S WORK ON IT! OK?

ONE ERROR I HEAR ALL THE TIME IS: "HER AND I WENT DOWNTOWN." HERE'S A WAY TO SEE IF THIS IS CORRECT.

her a

TAKE AWAY "AND I." — IS IT "HER WENT DOWNTOWN"? WHAT ABOUT "ME AND HIM"? TAKE AWAY "ME"...

her and I went downtown
me and him went downtown

SHE WENT DOWNTOWN! SHE AND I!

HE WENT DOWNTOWN, I WENT DOWN? TOWN... HE AND I WENT DOWN- TOWN!

GOOD WORK! NOW, MANY LAN- GUAGES PERMIT DOUBLE NEGATIVES. IN SPANISH, FOR EXAMPLE, "I NEVER DID NOTHING" IS CORRECT. IN ENGLISH, WE SAY....

I NEVER DID ANY- THING!

NOW, WHICH SENTENCES ARE CORRECT?

• I had spoke
• I had spoken
• It was broke
• It was broken
He done it
He did it
He has don

I DON'T GOT NO DOUGHNUTS? I DON'T HAVE ANY DOUGH- NUTS!

HE SHOULD HAVE DID IT? HE SHOULD HAVE **DONE** IT!!

did done
should would could

GOOD GRAMMAR IS DIFFICULT TO LEARN, BUT SOMEDAY THEY'LL THANK ME. WHAT KIND OF JOB CAN THEY EXPECT TO GET IF THEY CAN'T SPEAK THE LAN- GUAGE!

CLICK

"IT'S BRANDY AT ROCK'N CENTRAL, BEEN TALKIN' TO MIZZ CANDY RAPPER — HER AN' I GO 'WAY BACK! SHE'S GOTTA REAL BIG HIT: 'I SEEN YOU SWEATIN'!' —COMIN' UP GOOD ON THE CHARTS, Y'ALL!"

LIZ! PHONE'S FOR YOU!

THANKS.

HI, WARREN!...REALLY? BUT I THOUGHT YOU HAD THE WEEKEND OFF?....OH.

HOW LONG WILL YOU BE IN YELLOWKNIFE? WOW. SO, I GUESS I WON'T SEE YOU FOR A WHILE!

HEY, NO PROBLEM! WORK BEFORE PLEASURE!

TAKE CARE OF YOURSELF, OK? SEE YA!

CLICK

BWAPPBLFTT

WHO CALLED? WAS IT YOUR FRIEND WARREN? IS HE COMING TO SEE YOU?

MOTHER, DON'T ASK. DO NOT ASK.

IS HE COMING TO SEE YOU?

DO NOT ASK!

HE'S A NICE BOY, BUT INCONSISTENT. DON'T YOU THINK? HE CAN CANCEL A DATE AT THE LAST MINUTE AND IT DOESN'T SEEM TO BOTHER HIM.... DOES IT BOTHER YOU?

AAUGHH

I SHOULDN'T HAVE ASKED.

KEEP, KEEP, KEEP, KEEP...

CHUCK, CHUCK, CHUCK, CHUCK...

KEEP, TOSS, KEEP, CHUCK, CHUCK, KEEP, TOSS, KEEP...

TAKE TO APARTMENT

A ROLLING STONE GATHERS NO MESS!

ELIZABETH,... IF YOU AND A GUY WERE, YOU KNOW... "DOING STUFF" AND THE GUY TELLS HIS FRIENDS YOU WERE DOING A LOT **MORE** THAN YOU WERE DOING...

AND HIS FRIENDS START, YOU KNOW, LAUGHING AND STUFF, AN' THINKING YOU WERE, WELL... YOU KNOW.

I MEAN, IF YOU WEREN'T DOING STUFF AND HE SAID THAT YOU WERE, ...WHAT WOULD YOU DO?

I'D TELL HIM TO **STUFF IT !!!**

SO, TELL ME WHAT HAPPENED!

THE NIGHT THAT YOU ALL WENT TO MIKE'S PARTY? I WAS BABY-SITTING... AN' GERALD SHOWED UP.

HE HAD SOME WINE, AND WE WERE...UM, YOU KNOW.....JUST SORT OF....,WELL, NOTHING MUCH...

HE ALMOST GOT CAUGHT WHEN MOM AN' DAD CAME HOME! I SHOVED HIM OUT THE BACK DOOR, FILLED MY FACE WITH MOUTHWASH, AN' CALLED A CAB AFTER I GOT TO BED.

BUT WE DIDN'T **DO** ANYTHING! HONEST!

IT'S OK, APRIL. I BELIEVE YOU.

...WE DIDN'T HAVE **TIME!**

SO... WHAT SHOULD I DO ABOUT GERALD?

DO YOU STILL LIKE HIM?

I GUESS. BUT I'M MAD. AND WE'RE STILL IN THE BAND TOGETHER. ... I DUNNO.

ARE YOU THE KIND OF PERSON WHO CAN LET THINGS GO, GET ON WITH YOUR LIFE, AND JUST BE FRIENDS?

I DUNNO.

ARE YOU?

YES. YES, I AM.

BUT... IT'S REALLY, REALLY HARD.

For Better or For Worse

By Lynn Johnston

DR. PATTERSON? THE X-RAY DEVELOPER IS ON THE FRITZ.

OK. I'LL DEAL WITH IT.

AND MRS. FEGGMUTZ JUST CANCELLED HER 3-HOUR APPOINTMENT.

AGAIN.

CLOSE DOWN GENTLY, PLEASE.

CRUNCH!

*○✱#∅✱回

WE'VE JUST CRACKED THE CROWN.

WE'LL ORDER A REPLACEMENT AND I'LL PUT YOUR TEMPORARY BACK ON.

FIRST, I'LL REMOVE THE CEMENT FROM INSIDE IT....

BWEE EEE EEE EEE

PA-TWANNGG

★ @#∅ GLOVE IS CAUGHT IN THE DRILL AND I'VE LOST THE @!!✱ TEMPORARY!

GOOD THING WE FOUND THAT, OR I'D HAVE TO MAKE ANOTHER ONE! OK... I'M GOING TO ASK YOU TO CLOSE DOWN GENTLY, PLEASE. GENTLY!!

OF COURSE, IT DOESN'T FIT. I'LL HAVE TO DRILL IT OUT SOME MORE, THEN GRIND IT DOWN....

THERE! STACY WILL GET YOU A HOT TOWEL, AND WE'RE ALL DONE!

WHOA! WHAT AN AWFUL AFTERNOON! EVERYTHING THAT COULD GO WRONG... WENT WRONG!!

...IT'S A GOOD THING I WAS WORKING ON MY WIFE!

LYNN

CANDACE? OVER HERE!

HEY, LIZ—SORRY I'M LATE.

YOU'RE LOOKING WONDERFUL!

WOW! SO ARE YOU! I CAN'T BELIEVE YOU'RE HERE!

YOU LET YOUR HAIR GO BACK TO ITS NATURAL COLOR!

YEAH. THE BLACK WAS A LITTLE HARSH.

BUT YOU LOOKED COOL WITH BLACK HAIR!

I DID, DIDN'T I!

IT SEEMS LIKE A MILLION YEARS SINCE WE WERE ROOMMATES IN UNIVERSITY.

I KNOW. A LOT HAS HAPPENED SINCE THEN.

WE WERE SUCH KIDS, WEREN'T WE.

YEAH... WE WERE SO YOUNG!

SO, HAVE YOU GOT YOUR DRESS FOR SHAWNA-MARIE'S WEDDING?

YES. I PICKED IT UP THIS MORNING.

THE MATRON OF HONOR AND ALL THE BRIDESMAIDS ARE WEARING DIFFERENT PASTEL COLORS. THE BRIDE WILL BE IN "CREAM."

I'M GLAD I'M NOT IN THE WEDDING PARTY.

WHO ARE YOU INVITING?

WELL... I THOUGHT I'D INVITE ANTHONY. I MEAN, HE AND I AND SHAWNA-MARIE ALL WENT TO SCHOOL TOGETHER.

WHAT ABOUT PAUL?

THAT DIDN'T WORK OUT, CANDACE.

AND... WARREN?

HE'S JUST A FRIEND.

AND ANTHONY?

...I THOUGHT IT WAS TIME TO FIND OUT.

KNOCK-KNOCK! MAY I COME IN?

WELL, HELLO!! I DIDN'T EXPECT TO SEE YOU!!

ANTHONY, THIS IS A LOVELY OFFICE!

SURE IS! WHEN GORDON MADE ME A MANAGER, HE DID IT UP RIGHT!!

AND TO WHAT DO I OWE THE HONOR OF THIS MOST WELCOME VISIT?

WELL... SHAWNA-MARIE'S WEDDING IS COMING UP...

I KNOW. I GOT AN INVITATION.

GREAT! I'M IN THE WEDDING PARTY, AND I CAME TO SEE IF YOU'D BE MY "ESCORT"!

I'D LOVE TO, ELIZABETH!

IT'S JUST THAT.... I'VE INVITED SOMEONE ELSE.

AFTER THE TRIAL, WE BOTH GOT PRETTY BUSY. I KNEW THAT YOU'D BROKEN UP WITH PAUL AND WERE SEEING WARREN...

WARREN AND I AREN'T...

WE JUST HIRED A VERY NICE GIRL, ELIZABETH. SHE'S TAKEN MY PLACE IN ACCOUNTING. WE GET ALONG WELL...AND...I HAVE INVITED HER TO SHAWNA-MARIE'S WEDDING.

OTHERWISE....SURE.

HEY, NO PROBLEM! IT WAS JUST A THOUGHT! YOU KNOW, BECAUSE WE ALL WENT TO SCHOOL TOGETHER!

I GUESS I'LL SEE YOU THERE, THEN.

WOULD YOU LIKE ANOTHER COFFEE?

NO, THANKS.

I'D LIKE A HOLE TO CRAWL INTO WHERE I CAN **DIE!**

DUMB, DUMB, DUMB, DUMB! STUPID, STUPID, STUPID, STUPID!!!

OF COURSE ANTHONY RECEIVED AN INVITATION TO SHAWNA-MARIE'S WEDDING! **OF COURSE** HE'S GOING TO INVITE SOMEONE ELSE! HE'S NOT GOING TO HANG AROUND FOREVER WAITING FOR **ME!!**

HONK! HONNK!!

HEY, LADY! YOU GOT A GREEN LIGHT! WHAT'S WRONG WITH YOU?!!

I'M A TOTAL **IDIOT!!**

HI, SIS!

SNORT!

THUMP, THUMP, THUMP, THUMP, THUMP, THUMP!

AAAAUGHH!

P.M.S.?

NOPE.

M.E.N.

SIT DOWN, JIM, AND WE'LL GET UNDER WAY. YOUR CHARIOT AWAITS!

YES.

I'LL JUST GET YOU LOCKED IN AND WE'LL BE ALL SET TO GO.

GO!

LISTEN! HE SAID GO!!

JIM, YOU HAVEN'T SAID THAT WORD BEFORE! NOT IN ITS PROPER CONTEXT!—YOU'RE BEGINNING TO CONNECT THE RIGHT WORDS TO THE RIGHT MEANINGS! ISN'T THAT EXCITING?!!

BOXCAR!!!

WE'RE READY TO DO YOUR PHYSIO, JIM! AROUND TO THE LEFT!—YOU KNOW THE WAY!

YES.

NO SCENTS IS GOOD SENSE

LOTS OF TENSION IN YOUR LEGS. LET'S SEE IF WE CAN LIMBER THEM UP A BIT.

NOW, CAN YOU USE THE TECHNIQUE WE'VE BEEN PRACTICING? THAT'S RIGHT. ROLL TO A SITTING POSITION AND....GET OUT OF BED.

MMHH...

I ONCE RAN FOR MILES, CARRYING A RIFLE AND A GUNNY SACK ON MY BACK!

THIS IS HARDER.

I'M GOING TO CHECK YOUR BALANCE. DON'T LET ME PUSH YOU OVER, OK?

NO, NO.

GOOD WORK. ARE YOU READY TO WALK?

YES?

YES, WITH A CANE. —YOU CAN DO IT!

KEEP YOUR RIGHT FOOT ON THE RIGHT SIDE OF THE LINE. DON'T CROSS OVER. WE'RE GETTING THERE!...ONE STEP AT A TIME.

THAT'S WHAT I KEEP TELLING MYSELF. JIM'S GETTING BETTER... ONE STEP AT A TIME.

B...BUCKET ....YES? I KNOW. YOU DID A GREAT JOB TODAY, JIM! —WE'LL SEE YOU NEXT WEEK, OK?

AND, KEEP UP THE EXERCISES I GAVE YOU TO DO AT HOME.

YES?

YES. EVERY DAY.

THANKS, JUDITH. HE REALLY ENJOYS HIS PHYSIO DAYS.

WE HAVE OUR OWN LITTLE FAMILY OF FRIENDS IN HERE, DON'T WE!

—WE SURE DO!

THANK GOD FOR FAMILY AND FRIENDS!

YOUR SPEECH PATHOLOGIST IS COMING AT 3. MAYBE YOU SHOULD REST AWHILE.

I DON'T WANT TO REST.

YOU DON'T WANT TO REST? WOULD YOU LIKE TO LOOK AT THE PAPER AND HAVE SOME TEA?

YES.

YOUR FEET ARE SO COLD! I'LL GET YOUR SLIPPERS AND SOME WARMER SOCKS.

YOU'RE NOT READING THE PAPER. DON'T YOU WANT TO KNOW WHAT'S GOING ON IN THE WORLD?

YOU **ARE** MY WORLD.

NOW THAT SOMEONE'S WITH JIM... I MIGHT BE ABLE TO GO OUT FOR A WHILE.

I COULD VISIT A FRIEND, OR WALK TO THE CORNER STORE. ....OR SIT IN THE PARK AND WATCH THE PEOPLE GO BY.

IRIS, WE'RE FINE ON OUR OWN HERE. WHY DON'T YOU GO AND GET A LITTLE FRESH AIR!

THANKS, CHRISTINE. I THINK I WILL!

THERE'S NOTHING LIKE A COFFEE BREAK WHEN YOU'RE WORKING 24-7!

WE'RE GOING TO TRY THE WORD "I" AGAIN, JIM. THE SOUND IS IN "HIDE" AND "WIDE." WATCH MY MOUTH: "EYE."

AAEEEEHHH.

TRY IT AGAIN. LET'S USE THE PICTURE CARDS. THE ONE ON YOUR RIGHT HAS A SMILE ON IT. USE THE SMILE AS YOU SAY "EYE."

AHHH... EEEH.

GOOD. YOU HAVE THE "EE" SOUND. WATCH MY MOUTH AGAIN... "EYE"..."EYE."

EEEEH.

"EYE"..."EYE"..."EYE"... ARE YOU LOOKING AT ME?

YES.

I'M LOOKING YOU IN THE "EYES."

YOU'RE DOING THE "EEE" SOUND VERY WELL, JIM. LET'S PUT AN "M" IN FRONT OF IT, AND WE'LL HAVE THE WORD "ME."

TRY MEEE.

MMBUHHH.

AGAIN. WATCH MY MOUTH... "MEEE." MMM MMM UHEEEE.

AGAIN. "MEE."

EEEEEEEHHHHH WITH THE "M" SOUND: "MEE." MMM UUH HEEAAA.

ALMOST! AGAIN: MEEEE. MMMBBU HAAAAAA.

AAAA AUGH!

LET'S SAVE ME FOR A WHILE, OK?

LET'S SAVE BOTH OF US!!!

OK, COMPREHENSION EXERCISES! ARE YOU UP FOR IT? GOOD. ARE YOU A WOMAN?

NO.

ARE YOU A MAN?

YES.

IF YOU ARE A MAN, RAISE YOUR RIGHT HAND.

IF YOUR NAME IS JIM, RAISE YOUR LEFT HAND. IF YOU ARE SITTING DOWN, RAISE YOUR RIGHT HAND.

YOU CAN PUT YOUR HAND DOWN NOW, JIM...YOU CAN PUT YOUR HAND DOWN!

OH.

IRIS?!!!

WELL! I'M GLAD I CAME BACK FROM MY WALK WHEN I DID!

ME TOO!

JIM NEEDS SOME HELP WHEN HE'S IN THE WASHROOM, AND HE ISN'T COMFORTABLE GOING WITH ANYONE BESIDES MYSELF OR THE NURSES.

DON'T BE IN A RUSH TO GO, CHRISTINE. YOU CAN STAY FOR A WHILE.

IT'S OK, IRIS. WE'VE DONE ALL HIS SPEECH THERAPY FOR TODAY.

BUT... I NEED SOMEONE TO TALK TO!

I PUT INSTANT MASHED POTATO INTO THE SOUP, DEAR. IS IT EASIER TO EAT NOW?

BOXCAR. NOTHING BROKEN. TORQUING NUTS.

IS IT GOOD? WOULD YOU LIKE A NAPKIN? DID YOU HAVE A NICE DAY TODAY?

STANDARD SHIFT. STANDARD SHIFT.

JIM, THE QUESTIONS I'M ASKING ALL HAVE A "YES" OR "NO" ANSWER. YOU CAN SAY YES AND YOU CAN SAY NO!!! — DID YOU HAVE A NICE DAY TODAY?

IF YOUR LOVED ONE RESPONDS WITH MEANINGLESS OR UNKIND WORDS, DO NOT TAKE IT PERSONALLY. THIS IS ALL PART OF LIVING WITH APHASIA.

≈SNIFF≈ WHAT A STRANGE CONDITION THIS IS. ....AT LEAST IT COMES WITH A MANUAL.

WHEN HE'S SLEEPING, HE JUST LOOKS LIKE MY JIM. —AS IF HE'D NEVER HAD A STROKE AT ALL.

I WONDER IF HE CAN SPEAK NORMALLY IN HIS DREAMS. I WONDER IF HE CAN RUN AND WALK AGAIN AND DO ALL THE THINGS HE USED TO DO.

I WONDER HOW MUCH HE KNOWS, HOW MUCH HE REMEMBERS AND UNDERSTANDS. IT'S SO HARD TO TELL WHEN HE CAN'T COMMUNICATE PROPERLY.

JIM... I HOPE YOU KNOW.... THAT I LOVE YOU.

AND LADY... I AM **CRAZY** ABOUT YOU!!

YOU'VE DECIDED THEN, FOR SURE. WE'VE MADE ALL THE ARRANGEMENTS, APRIL. WE'RE GOING TO MOVE DOWN THE STREET.

I WANTED THAT HOUSE TO BE MICHAEL'S. IT'S BETTER THIS WAY, HONEY. OUR HOUSE IS THE PERFECT SIZE FOR HIS FAMILY, AND IT'S TOO BIG FOR US.

WE KNOW YOU'RE UPSET. WE HADN'T PLANNED TO MOVE UNTIL YOU WERE IN UNIVERSITY. ...THIS JUST HAPPENED TO COME ALONG, AND WE COULDN'T PASS UP SUCH A GREAT OPPORTUNITY.

YOU'LL GET USED TO LIVING IN A NEW HOUSE. WE CAN FINISH THE BASEMENT—JUST FOR YOU!

NOW THAT I'VE MADE MY MIND UP, JOHN... I CAN'T WAIT TO MOVE IN. YES... WE'RE GOING TO ENJOY THIS PLACE.

WE DID IT. WE'VE BOUGHT A SMALLER HOUSE—AND THE KIDS ARE GOING TO TAKE OURS!

THIS WAS THE RIGHT DECISION, ELLY. I KNOW. I'VE SAID MANY TIMES THAT OUR HOUSE WAS TOO BIG FOR JUST THE TWO OF US.

EVERYTHING'S NICELY FALLING INTO PLACE. CRAAAAACKKKK!

THUMMPP!!

WHAT HAPPENED?! A BIRCH TREE FELL ON THE HOUSE!

DON'T WORRY—IT'S PROBABLY MINOR DAMAGE. BUT... WE JUST BOUGHT THIS PLACE!

I'M... I'M IN SHOCK! THINGS LIKE THIS HAPPEN. WE'LL DEAL WITH IT.

THERE'S PLASTER ALL OVER THE LIVING ROOM... AND WE HAVEN'T EVEN MOVED IN YET! THAT'S A GOOD THING!

EVERYTHING'S GOING TO BE OK, HONEY. HOW CAN YOU BE SO POSITIVE, WHEN I'M SO ANGRY?!!!

OPPOSITES ATTRACT.

REALLY? WHOA! THAT'S TERRIBLE! SURE, I'LL GET IT GASSED UP AND READY.

WHAT?!

MY FOLKS JUST GOT THE KEYS TO MR. STIBBS' HOUSE—WHEN A TREE FELL ON IT!

DAD'S COMING TO GET THE CHAIN SAW. I'LL GO AND GIVE HIM A HAND.

A TREE FELL ON THE HOUSE?!!

IT'S AN OMEN! THIS WHOLE CHANGING HOUSES THING IS... CURSED! I NEVER WANTED MY PARENTS TO MOVE—I EVEN **PRAYED** THAT SOMETHING WOULD HAPPEN TO STOP THEM!!

IT'S ALL **MY** FAULT!!!

SHOULDN'T TAKE MORE THAN A DAY OR TWO TO FIX THE HOUSE, DAD. I'VE GOT SOME GUYS COMING OVER TO CHECK IT OUT.

THAT REMINDS ME. THERE ARE THINGS THAT NEED REPAIRING OVER AT YOUR PLACE.

YOU MEAN, **YOUR** PLACE!

YOU AND DEANNA OWN THAT HOUSE NOW.

WE WON'T OWN THAT HOUSE FOR A LONG TIME, JOHN. IT'S GOING TO OWN **US!**

IT'S NICE TO HAVE A SENSE OF "BELONGING," ISN'T IT.

I FEEL SO GUILTY, EVA.

APRIL, YOU HAD NOTHING TO DO WITH A TREE FALLING ON A HOUSE YOUR PARENTS BOUGHT.

I DIDN'T WANT THEM TO MOVE. I WANTED MY BROTHER TO MOVE. I WANTED TO STAY HERE....IN MY ROOM, IN MY HOUSE. I PUT A CURSE ON THAT PLACE!

REALLY.

I PRAYED THAT SOMETHING WOULD HAPPEN TO KEEP THEM HERE—AND THEN THE TREE FALLS!

WELL, THERE'S NO SUCH THING AS CURSES, OK?

...IT WAS AN ACT OF GOD.

DO YOU THINK I'M WEIRD, EVA?

NOPE. IF YOU'RE WEIRD, THEN I'M WEIRD, TOO!

I FEEL, LIKE, TOTALLY ALONE SOMETIMES. NOBODY UNDERSTANDS ME. NOBODY LISTENS, NOBODY CARES... I DON'T EVEN THINK THAT GERALD DOES!

YEAH.... GERALD.

DID YOU KNOW THAT HE'S AGREED TO DO A GIG WITH BECKY?

WHAT?!!

THAT'S, LIKE, TREASON'! WHAT WOULD MAKE HIM COMMIT TREASON?!!

150 BUCKS, AND A CHANCE TO BE SEEN ON TELEVISION.

OH.

SO, YOU HAVE THE KEYS TO THE STIBBS' HOUSE! WHEN DO YOU MOVE?

NOT FOR A WHILE, CONNIE— BUT I'VE BEEN PACKING!

GEORGE STILL HAS TO REMOVE SOME OF HIS FURNITURE, AND THERE ARE REPAIRS TO BE DONE.

I'M GLAD WE'LL STILL BE NEIGHBOURS, ELLY.

ME TOO.

HOW DO MIKE AND DEANNA FEEL ABOUT BUYING THEIR FIRST HOUSE? ARE THEY EXCITED?

I'D SAY THEY'RE TAKING IT IN STRIDE.

HOW LONG DO YOU WANT TO KEEP RUNNING?

'TIL I'M TOO TIRED TO THINK!

WOW. WE ACTUALLY BOUGHT MY PARENTS' HOUSE, DEE.

YES, WE DID.

SOMEHOW, I JUST CAN'T GET MY HEAD AROUND IT.

MAYBE THAT'S BECAUSE YOUR FOLKS AND APRIL ARE STILL LIVING THERE.

ONCE WE HAVE IT ALL TO OURSELVES, WE CAN CHANGE THE CARPETING, UPDATE THE CABINETS, PAINT ALL THE ROOMS, VARNISH THE HARDWOOD, PUT IN NEW APPLIANCES, NEW DRAPES, ... AND THEN, WE'LL FEEL LIKE IT TRULY BELONGS TO US!!!

ANIMALS JUST MARK THEIR TERRITORY. ....HUMANS HAVE TO REDECORATE.

I WANNA KNOW WHAT'S GOING ON WITH BECKY AN' GERALD, EVA.

I TOLD YOU ALL I KNOW....

HER DRUMMER ISN'T AVAILABLE FOR THIS THING SHE'S DOING AT THE MALL, SO SHE ASKED GERALD TO FILL IN.

HMPH.

SO, HE'S GONNA SLITHER OVER TO "THE OTHER SIDE."

IT'S JUST A TELETHON, APRIL.

IT'S NOT LIKE SHE ASKED HIM TO GO ON THE ROAD.

OH, I'D ASK HIM TO GO ON THE ROAD, ALRIGHT.

THEN... I'D STOMP ALL OVER HIM.

I DUNNO WHY YOU'RE SO TICKED AT ME, MAN! I WAS JUST KIDDING AROUND WHEN I TOLD THE GUYS ABOUT "PARTY NIGHT."

NOTHING "HAPPENED" THAT NIGHT, GERALD, AND YOU KNOW IT! BUT—YOU LET PEOPLE THINK...

HEY!! RELAX! WE'RE A COUPLE!

...REMEMBER?

I DON'T THINK SO!—YOU LIED ABOUT ME... AN' NOW, YOU'RE GONNA PLAY DRUMS FOR BECKY!!

BUT... THAT'S JUST A ONE-NIGHT STAND!

GOOD!..... I HOPE SHE CAN ONLY STAND YOU FOR ONE NIGHT.

APRIL, IF YOU AN' GERALD AREN'T SPEAKING TO EACH OTHER, WHAT'S GONNA HAPPEN TO THE BAND?

I DUNNO.

YOU GOTTA THINK OF THE REST OF US, MAN. YOU'RE LEAD GUITAR!

WE'LL CONTINUE ON A PROFESSIONAL LEVEL.

WHEN YOU'RE ON A PROFESSIONAL LEVEL, YOU DON'T HAFTA BE "FRIENDS." YOU JUST CONCENTRATE ON THE MUSIC. SO—EVERYTHING WILL BE TOTALLY PROFESSIONAL FROM NOW ON.

MIND IF I HAVE LUNCH WITH YOU GUYS?

HMPH!

MIND IF I LEAVE?

COOL MOVE THERE, APRIL!..... VERY PROFESSIONAL.

For Better or For Worse
By Lynn Johnston

90

I THOUGHT YOU WEREN'T GONNA GO FOR A BASEMENT APARTMENT, LIZ.

I WAS IN A RUSH, IT WAS AVAILABLE, THE RENT'S OK, IT'S CLOSE TO WORK AND IT'S FURNISHED.

THEN, IT'S ...COZY!

IS THIS THE DRESS?

YEAH. I'M VIOLET, DAWN IS AQUA, ALYSSA IS YELLOW AND JEN IS GREEN.

...A VERITABLE PASTEL RAINBOW!

IT'S SO WE CAN ALL SHOW UP AT SOME FUNCTION LATER... WEARING THE SAME DRESS, AND NO ONE WILL KNOW WE WERE BRIDESMAIDS.

YEAH. RIGHT.

SO, ARE YOU GOING WITH ANTHONY?

NO, HE'S INVITED SOMEONE ELSE.

THEN, YOU DON'T HAVE A DATE FOR THIS THING?

IT'LL BE EASIER THAT WAY, CANDACE. I'LL BE FREE TO HELP OUT, GET STUFF ORGANIZED—REALLY BE USEFUL!

MMM.

THEY'VE PUT A LOT OF EFFORT INTO THIS WEDDING. WHEN IT'S OUTDOORS, A LOT CAN GO WRONG.

SHAWNA-MARIE'S ALL WORRIED ABOUT RAIN AND THE CATERING AND THE DECORATIONS, —SHE'S A TOTAL WRECK RIGHT NOW.

YEAH?

THE WAY I SEE IT.... AS LONG AS THE GROOM AND THE MINISTER SHOW UP, —THERE'S NO PROBLEM!

DO YOU THINK YOU AND RUDY WILL EVER TIE THE KNOT, CANDACE?

I DUNNO. WE KINDA LIKE THINGS THE WAY THEY ARE.

I MEAN, WE'RE LEGALLY RESPONSIBLE FOR OUR RELATIONSHIP ANYWAY.... SO, WHY MAKE A PUBLIC DECLARATION OF OUR LOVE?

TRADITION!!!

ELIZABETH, NOBODY'S GONNA MAKE ME SHOVE THESE BONES INTO A FLOUNCY WHITE WEDDING DRESS, JUST FOR THE SAKE OF TRADITION !!! —AND YOU?

.... I'D DO IT FOR MY MOM.

LET'S GO OVER THE REHEARSAL ONCE MORE. ....MUSICIANS ARE HERE, THEY PLAY UNTIL ALL GUESTS ARE SEATED.

THE MINISTER WILL ENTER FROM THIS SIDE, THE GROOM AND BEST MAN WILL TURN TO THEIR LEFT AS THE MUSIC COMMENCES AND THE BRIDESMAIDS WILL THEN APPEAR.

ALL WILL STAND, PROCESSION COMMENCES, WEDDING PARTY WILL STOP AT THE FRONT, AND TURN. **THEN,** THE BRIDE WILL MAKE HER ENTRANCE.

MOM?

I KNOW YOU WANT ALL CLASSICAL MUSIC, MOM... BUT I'D REALLY LIKE TO WALK DOWN THE AISLE TO A MODERN PIECE THAT I LIKE!

WE CAN'T HAVE SOME SILLY **LOVE** SONG HERE, SHAWNA-MARIE! THIS IS A **WEDDING**!!

THIS HAPPENED AT MY BROTHER'S WEDDING, DAWN. DEANNA'S MOTHER CONTROLLED THE WHOLE THING.

IT'S BEEN CRAZY FROM THE BEGINNING, LIZ! ....HASSLES WITH THE DRESS, HASSLES WITH THE MUSIC AND THE FOOD, HASSLES ABOUT THE LOCATION....

SHAWNA FINALLY GAVE UP AND LET HER MOM DO WHATEVER SHE WANTED!

WHOA... HAVEN'T THE BRIDE AND GROOM MADE **ANY** DECISIONS ON THEIR OWN?

YEAH...

WHEN IT'S ALL OVER—THEY'RE MOVING.

OOPS, IT LOOKS LIKE THE BRIDE IS STRESSING OUT AGAIN. TIME FOR THE MAID OF HONOR TO STEP IN!

LET ME TAKE YOUR PLATE.

EXCUSE ME.... ARE YOU ELIZABETH?

YES?

MY NAME IS MASON—I'M THE BEST MAN. AND, UM... SINCE NEITHER OF US IS BRINGING A GUEST TO THE WEDDING, THE GROOM ASKED ME TO BE YOUR ESCORT TOMORROW.

SURE. THAT WOULD BE FINE!

SOMETHING TELLS ME THIS FAMILY FIASCO MIGHT BE FUN AFTER ALL!!

BRIDESMAIDS? THE CARS ARE HERE! HUSTLE, PEOPLE!

MAID OF HONOR, THE BRIDE NEEDS HELP WITH HER VEIL!

YOU LOOK BEAUTIFUL, SHAWNA-MARIE! .... HOW ARE YOU HOLDING UP?

FINE, THANKS, LIZ .....

YOU SHOULD SEE THE CORSET I'M WEARING UNDER THIS DRESS!

SHAWNA-MARIE, DAWN AND I ALWAYS WONDERED WHICH ONE OF US WOULD BE MARRIED FIRST....

SHAWNA'S FIRST, DAWN AND DAVID ARE ENGAGED TO BE MARRIED NEXT YEAR. SHE'S ASKED ME TO BE A BRIDESMAID AT HER WEDDING, TOO.

WE'VE KNOWN EACH OTHER SINCE GRADE SCHOOL... AND IT'S GREAT TO SHARE THESE VERY PERSONAL MOMENTS.

WEDDINGS ARE .... FULL OF VERY PERSONAL MOMENTS.

ELIZABETH!

YOU MAY NOW KISS THE BRIDE!

CONGRATULATIONS!!

LOVELY WEDDING, DEAR!

YOU LOOK BEAUTIFUL.

GOOD LUCK!

ELIZABETH, I'D LIKE YOU TO MEET JULIA.

ANTHONY'S TOLD ME SO MUCH ABOUT YOU!

REALLY?

OH, YEAH! AN' GUESS WHAT! YOUR DAD IS MY DENTIST! CHECK OUT HIS HANDIWORK!

HE JUST TOOK OUT AN IMPACTED ONE... WAY AT THE BACK. HE CALLED IT "AN INCONVENIENT TOOTH."

SO, YOU TWO HAVE BEEN FRIENDS FOREVER, RIGHT? I DON'T KNOW A SOUL HERE, REALLY—EXCEPT FOR THE CATERER. I DID THEIR BOOKS FOR A WHILE.

ELIZABETH!! THERE YOU ARE.

MASON!

COME ON! THEY'RE GETTING THE BRIDAL PARTY TOGETHER FOR PICTURES! LET'S GO!

AND...I WANT YOU TO STAND AS CLOSE TO ME AS POSSIBLE!

ANTHONY—WOULD YOU LIKE SOME PUNCH?

NO, THANKS, JULIA. I'VE JUST HAD ONE.

ANTHONY LOOKS SO DIFFERENT! HE'S SHAVED OFF HIS MUSTACHE AND CHANGED HIS GLASSES.

HE LOOKS LIKE THE ANTHONY I REMEMBER. HE LOOKS LIKE THE BOY I USED TO DATE; THE ONE I'VE ALWAYS CARED FOR.

WHAT'S WRONG, ELIZABETH? YOU STOPPED DEAD IN YOUR TRACKS!

IS THERE A PROBLEM?

YES!

MASON, I'M STUCK. I NEED YOUR HELP.

HEY—JUST ASK!

NEVER WEAR HEELS TO A GARDEN PARTY!

AS YOUR FRIEND, ANTHONY, I'VE GOTTA TELL YOU.... THAT GIRL YOU'RE SO CRAZY ABOUT STILL CARES!

MAYBE.

WHAT "MAYBE"? OF COURSE SHE DOES! SEE THE WAY SHE LOOKS AT YOU?

I THINK YOU SHOULD MAKE A MOVE.

REALLY?!!

ABSOLUTELY. IF YOU WANT THAT GIRL, TODAY IS THE DAY TO TELL HER SO.

BUT JULIA, SHE'S WITH THE BEST MAN!

YOU'RE BETTER.

WHAT HAPPENED TO MY COFFEE CUP?

UM.... I THINK I SOLD IT.

APRIL, YOU DIDN'T PUT THE GARDEN TOOLS IN THE YARD SALE, DID YOU?

OOPS.

HAS ANYONE SEEN THE CALCULATOR?

DOES SHE COME WITH THE CHAIR?

HEY...APRIL...HOWYA DOIN'?

OK, I GUESS.

APRIL...I...WAN...NA...TELL...YOU...SOME...THING! THERE'S GONNA...BE...A...TEL...E...THON AT THE MALL...WITH...LIVE...MU...SIC...AN' EVERY...THING!

I KNOW.

MY SO-CALLED BOYFRIEND IS PLAYING DRUMS FOR REBECCA.

ARE...YOU...GOING?

I DUNNO...WHY?

BE...CAUSE...THE TELE...THON'S FOR...

US!!

YES WE CAN...YES WE CAN

SPECIAL EDUCATION

LEARNING CENTER

THE...TEL...E...THON...AT THE...MALL IS...FOR US,...APRIL!...KIDS...WITH...SPECIAL NEEDS.

I DIDN'T KNOW THAT!

SPECIAL EDU

RE...BE...CCA...IS...SINGING FOR FREE...AN'...THERE...WILL...BE...DAN...CERS...AN' MAGIC...AN' IT WILL...GO FOR...24 HOURS!

YOUR...BAND...COULD...BE...THERE!...THEY...WANT...EVERY...ONE TO PAR...TISSS...I...PATE!

NO. I DON'T WANT TO BE ON THE SAME STAGE AS BECKY AND GERALD.

THEN...IT'S NO...PROB...LEM, MAN!...THERE'S GONNA BE...TWO...STAGES!!

OH.

WOULD...YOU...WANNA...HAVE LUNCH...WITH...ME?

SURE, SHANNON. WHY NOT?

YOU...KNOW...SOME OF MY...FRIENDS, RIGHT?

HI.

HELLO!

H'LO!

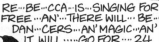
today's specials
pita salad
veggie wrap
chicken...
stea...
SOUP
Tomato
Bean w...
...cken
...ris't

WE WERE IN THE SAME HOME ECONOMICS CLASS! REMEMBER, JACK? YOU LEARNED HOW TO COOK EGGS!

EGGS! I COOKED EGGS ALL BY MYSELF!

HEY, APRIL! – I SEE YOU'RE SITTING WITH THE "EGG HEADS"!

BANG BANG BANG BANG!!

QUIET, EVERYONE! SHANNON LAKE WANTS TO SAY SOMETHING!

I···WANT···TO SAY···STOP! ···STOP···MA···KING···FUN OF···US! ···WE'RE DIF'RENT FROM···YOU···BUT, ···SO WHAT?!!

DON'T···GIVE···US A··· HARD···TIME···· GIVE US···A CHANCE!

YOU···TEASE···ME ABOUT··· THE···WAY···I···TALK! ··· I···WAS···BORN···WITH A··· CLEFT···PALATE! ···THEY COULDN'T···FIX··· IT····UNTIL···I··· WAS···FOUR!

I···HAD···TO LEARN···HOW TO···SPEAK···ALL···OVER AGAIN···AND···THAT···IS··· WHY···I···TALK LIKE··· THIS.

I CAN'T·····CHANGE···THE WAY····I···TALK···

BUT···YOU···CAN CHANGE···THE···· WAY···YOU··· LISTEN!!

KIDS···WITH····SPECIAL NEEDS ARE···PEOPLE···TOO! ···WE··· HAVE A···LOT···TO···OFFER! GET···TO KNOW···US! ···DON'T··· TEASE···US!

PLEASE!··· E·NOUGH·· IS··E·NOUGH!

WOOHOOO!! YAH! YESSS! CLAP CLAP CLAP CLAP CLAP CLAP

100

SHANNON, THAT WAS THE BEST SPEECH **EVER!!**
YEAH!
YOU GO, GIRL!
YES!

WHOA!... I'M...SHA... KING!...THAT TOOK... GUTS,...MAN!
GUTS!

HEY, WE'RE REALLY SORRY. WE'VE SAID SOME STUFF THAT WAS TOTALLY OUT OF LINE.

WAY TO GO, SHANNON.
YEAH. WE REALLY NEEDED TO HEAR THAT.

KNOW WHAT,... APRIL? ....MAY... BE... I... WAS BORN...DIF'RENT...SO I COULD...MAKE A...DIFFER-....ENCE.

GERALD?
I THOUGHT YOU WEREN'T SPEAKING TO ME.
WELL, I AM.

OUR BAND SHOULD DO THE TELETHON. I DON'T CARE IF YOU ARE PLAYING DRUMS FOR REBECCA... IT'S FOR A GOOD CAUSE.
COOL!

FRIENDS AGAIN?

MORE THAN FRIENDS AGAIN!

WHATCHA GONNA DO THIS SUMMER, APRIL?
GO BACK TO THE FARM.

STILL THINK YOU'D LIKE TO BE A VET-ERINARIAN?
YEAH. IT FEELS RIGHT TO ME.

WHAT FEELS RIGHT FOR YOU, EVA?
I'M NOT SURE... BUT SINCE I'VE BEEN IN THE BAND, I'VE FOUND OUT THAT I GOTTA KEEP SINGING!

'BYE, APRIL.
GOODBYE, SHANNON.

LIFE IS LIKE CHRIST-MAS — WHEN YOU THINK ALL THE BOXES HAVE BEEN OPENED ....YOU DISCOVER ANOTHER GIFT.

AN' I GUESS THAT'S ALL I GOTTA SAY ABOUT MY GOOD BUDDY, HERE. YOU MARRIED A BEAUTIFUL GIRL, MAN!

TINK TINK TINK TINK TINK TINK TINK TINK

TO WIND UP, I GOTTA SAY—MAY YOU LIVE IN PEACE AN' HARMONY AND HAVE LOTS OF KIDS!

Brian and Shawna-Marie

SHAWNA-MARIE, WHEN WE WALKED DOWN THE AISLE TODAY, I SAID TO MYSELF (SNIFF) MY LITTLE GIRL IS A BRIDE. SHE'S ALL GROWN UP!

Shawna-Marie

OK, MASTER OF CEREMONIES—YOU CAN WRAP UP THE DINNER AND START THE DANCE.

MASON?

SNOZZZ

MAY I?

YOU MAY.

YOUR DATE WON'T MIND?

MY "DATE" WON'T CARE!

Z

AND...YOURS?

I DON'T THINK SO.

I'VE BEEN WANTING TO DANCE WITH YOU FOR A LONG TIME, ELIZABETH.

JUST DANCE?

JUST...... EVERYTHING.

OK, EVERYONE! WE'RE GONNA FORM A CONGA LINE!!!

WHERE ARE WE GOING?

SOMEWHERE PRIVATE, WHERE WE CAN TALK!

OR.....NOT SAY ANYTHING AT ALL.

YOUR NEW HOUSE ISN'T SO BAD, APRIL! MY ROOM'S SMALLER, AN' I HAFTA SHARE THE CAN WITH MY FOLKS.

AWW, POOR BABY! ANYWAYS, YOU'LL BE GOING AWAY TO UNIVERSITY, SO IT WON'T MATTER!

IT WILL MATTER. THIS ISN'T THE HOUSE I'M USED TO. IT'S NOT "HOME."

WHAT IF YOU LIVED IN A WAR ZONE AND YOUR HOUSE WAS GONE AN' ALL YOU HAD LEFT WAS YOUR FAMILY! YOU'D CONSIDER YOURSELF LUCKY, WOULDN'T YOU?

THIS ISN'T A WAR ZONE, EVA.

CONSIDER YOURSELF LUCKY.

FACE IT, GIRL! YOU GOT IT GOOD! IF YOU'D STAYED AT YOUR OLD HOUSE, YOU'D BE LOOKING AFTER YOUR BROTHER'S KIDS ALL THE TIME!

TRUE.

HERE, YOU'VE GOT A NICE ROOM AND THE POSSIBILITY OF SCORING AN APARTMENT DOWNSTAIRS!

THAT'S THE IDEA, RIGHT? THEY WANNA TURN THE BASEMENT INTO YOUR PRIVATE SPACE! HOW COOL IS THAT?!!

PRETTY COOL, I GUESS.

I GUESS?!! GIRL, YOU ARE SO TOTALLY SPOILED ROTTEN!!

EVA, I AM **NOT** SPOILED ROTTEN!!

WHAT ARE YOU DOING?

LOOKING FOR YOUR "BEST BEFORE" DATE.

EVA'S GOING HOME ALREADY? HOW COME?

WE HAD A SLIGHT DIFFERENCE OF OPINION.... ABOUT THIS HOUSE.

HONEY, COME HERE.

DON'T TOUCH ME!! YOU DON'T KNOW HOW I FEEL! **YOU DON'T UNDERSTAND!**

YOU'RE NOT HAVING A GOOD TIME RIGHT NOW. THIS MOVE HAS BEEN VERY HARD ON YOU. WE'VE TURNED YOUR WORLD UPSIDE DOWN!

YOU'RE HURT. YOU'RE CONFUSED AND YOU'RE ANGRY.... AND YOU HAVE EVERY RIGHT TO BE SO.

RATS.

... SHE UNDERSTANDS.

106

Panel 1: JUST GETTING THE LAST COAT DONE, MRS. P. —GOOD THING THAT TREE FELL ON THIS PLACE — YOUR ATTIC WAS FULL OF SQUIRRELS!

Panel 2: WHEN WE OPENED HER UP, WE FOUND QUITE A NEST OF 'EM. THE MOTHBALLS WE THREW IN SHOULD KEEP 'EM FROM COMING BACK.

Panel 3: OF COURSE, THE MOTHBALLS WILL STINK' YOUR PLACE UP A BIT — BUT... THAT'S THE PRICE YOU PAY FOR PRIVACY!

Panel 4: AND HERE'S THE PRICE YOU PAY FOR **ME**!

LYNN

Panel 5: :SNIFFF:.... WHAT'S THAT SMELL?

MOTHBALLS. THE ROOF REPAIR GUYS PUT THEM IN THE ATTIC TO GET RID OF THE SQUIRRELS.

Panel 6: SQUIRRELS?! YEAH... AN' THE SUMP PUMP IS BORKED, SO MOM WENT TO GET A NEW ONE.

Panel 7: DID YOU NOTICE THE SQUEEK IN THE HALLWAY? THERE ARE CARPENTER ANTS IN THE PORCH SUPPORTS, AN' IT LOOKS LIKE THE FRIDGE COMPRESSOR IS GOING.

WHAT?

EEEKAH SKWEEKA

Panel 8: STIBBS SAID THAT FRIDGE WAS **NEW!**

NEW HOUSE.... NEW HASSLES.

LYNN

Panel 9: GIVE ME A HAND WITH THIS AREA RUG, APRIL.

I THINK I'D BETTER VACUUM THE FLOOR FIRST, DAD.

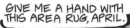

Panel 10: I FOUND THE UTENSILS, HONEY. COULD YOU CLEAN THEM OFF TOO?

SCRUB SCRAPE SKRUB SKRITT

Panel 11: I'VE UNPACKED THE LAST BOX, MOM — AN' I WASHED THE FRONT WINDOWS.

GOOD. I THINK WE'RE FINISHED. EVERYTHING'S BEEN CLEANED AND FIXED AND TAKEN CARE OF.

Panel 12: WE'RE COMPLETELY MOVED IN. WE CAN FINALLY CALL THIS PLACE "OURS."

YEAH!

Panel 13: HOME SWEAT HOME !!

LYNN

DO YOU THINK YOUR MOM WILL MIND IF WE REMOVE HER WALLPAPER?

IT'S OUR HOUSE NOW, DEE!

WE CAN DO ANYTHING WE WANT TO DO: PAINT, VARNISH, PAPER, CARPET, TILE...

I KNOW. I'M JUST SENSITIVE ABOUT HER FEELINGS. YOUR PARENTS LIVED HERE FOR A LONG TIME.

DO YOU THINK SHE WOULD MIND IF WE REDESIGNED THE KITCHEN?

YOU WANT TO CHANGE THE KITCHEN?

BUT... I'VE ALWAYS LIKED IT THE WAY IT **IS!**

MUM, MUM, MUM, MUMMM... COME HERE, YOU!

ROBIN, WHAT'S IN YOUR MOUTH? OPEN UP. GIVE IT TO MOMMY.

GAAH.

A TACK?! WHERE DID YOU FIND A **TACK**?

TACK!

HAH!.....LOOKS LIKE THE ONE I STUCK IN THE BACK WALL OF THE UP-STAIRS CLOSET!

WHAT DID YOU DO THAT FOR?

I DUNNO... IT'S BEEN THERE SINCE I WAS NINE.

MOM, CAN WE LOOK AT THESE?

NOT NOW, HONEY. I HAVE CLEANING TO DO.

PLEASE? I WANNA SEE THE PHOTOGRAPHS.

FO-GRAFFS! FO-GRAFFS!

NOT NOW!

WE'LL LOOK AT THEM TO-GETHER AFTER I'VE FIN-ISHED MY WORK, OK? WE'LL LOOK AT THEM LATER!

RATTLE... RUMBLE ROLL...

CRASH!

UM... WE'LL LOOK AT THEM NOW.

109

FOR BETTER OR FOR WORSE

By Lynn Johnston

HOW DOES IT FEEL TO BE GOING OUT WITH A GUY WHO HAS A CHILD, ELIZABETH?

WONDERFUL.

I MEAN—THIS CAN REALLY COMPLICATE A RELATIONSHIP.

ANTHONY...

BEING WITH YOU AND FRANCIE ....IS A WALK IN THE PARK.

PUT YOUR HANDS TOGETHER FOR OUR VERY OWN... REBECCA!!

TELETHON

FOLKS! KEEP THOSE PHONES RINGING, KEEP THE DONATIONS ROLLING IN! — THIS IS HOUR 4 OF THE GREAT "HEARTS TOGETHER TELETHON!"

GERALD, YOU WERE... GREAT!

THANKS! YOU'RE ON NEXT! —GO FOR IT!!

#2

THIS IS A SONG WE WROTE — IT'S CALLED "EVERYBODY'S DIFFERENT."

ELETH

BUT...DEEP DOWN INSIDE...WE'RE REALLY ALL THE SAME.

EVERYBODY'S DIFFERENT, THERE'S NO 2 OF A KIND! WE'RE DIFFERENT SHAPES AN' COLORS—AN' WE'VE GOT DIFFERENT MINDS...

THERE'S A DIFFERENCE IN OUR FACES, JUST 'CAUSE THAT'S WHO WE ARE—AN' WE LIVE IN DIFFERENT PLACES, SOME ARE NEAR, SOME ARE FAR—

IF WE'RE THE HIGHEST ON THE FOOD CHAIN, THE ONES WITH THE BRAINS....WHY DO WE ACT SO INSANE?!

WHAT DO YOU THINK OF THEM, REBECCA?

THEY'RE GOOD. THEY'RE REALLY GOOD.

THAT'S A COMPLIMENT!!

THAT'S THE TRUTH.

APRIL...YOU GUYS...WERE AWE...SOME!!

THANKS, SHANNON!

NICE WORK, LADIES!

BECKY! I DIDN'T THINK YOU'D STAY AND LISTEN!

COOL!

WELL, SOMETIMES... I DON'T LISTEN ENOUGH.

...YOU GUYS ROCKED! I'D KEEP YOUR DRUMMER, BUT I'D HATE TO SPLIT UP YOUR BAND!

HOO! TONIGHT WAS A BLAST!

WANT TO HANG OUT BEFORE MY NEXT SET?

I THOUGHT YOU WERE TOO GOOD TO HANG OUT WITH US.

EVA!!!

KNOW WHAT?.... MAYBE I WAS TOO GOOD FOR MY OWN GOOD.

APRIL! WANNA COME OUTSIDE AN' SEE WHAT I'M DOING WITH MY TRAINS?

NO THANKS, DAD... I'M ON A ROLL!

YOU'VE GOTTA SEE MY NEW WORKSHOP. I'VE GOT IT ALL ORGANIZED!

OK. ...MAYBE LATER.

HEY, MIKE! WANNA CHECK OUT MY NEW LAYOUT?

OH. OK. SURE. I'LL CALL TO-MORROW........'BYE.

STEVE! - IT'S JOHN PATTERSON! WHAT? HEY - NO PROBLEM! GO FOR IT!

...GET A HOLE IN ONE OUT THERE, BUDDY!

DAVE! WANNA COME OVER? NO?

WELL.... SAY "HI!" TO THE GRAND-KIDS FOR ME!

WHAT'S THE MATTER, HONEY?

≶SNORT≶

....I'VE GOT NOBODY TO PLAY WITH.

THANKS FOR COMING TO PICK US UP, POP! THE TELETHON'S STILL GOING, BUT WE'RE WASTED!

NO PROBLEM!

...I'M ALWAYS AWAKE AT 4 A.M.

WE WATCHED YOUR DUET ON TELEVISION, AND YOUR MOM CALLED IN A PLEDGE OF 50 BUCKS!

WE MADE SOME MONEY, EVA!

YEP! YOU TWO SANG LIKE THERE'S NO TOMORROW!

DAD...THERE **IS** NO TO-MORROW!

IT'S ALREADY **TODAY**!!

THANKS FOR THE RIDE, DR. P! HAVE A GOOD TRIP OUT WEST, APRIL!

BYE, EVA!

BECKY CAME AND TALKED TO ME AT THE TELETHON, DAD. WE WENT TO THE FOOD COURT FOR COFFEE. SHE TALKED ABOUT HER BAND. SHE TALKED ABOUT HER FATHER. AS HER MANAGER, HE'S ARROGANT AND CONTROLLING.

HE WON'T SPEAK TO HER MOM...AND HE'S JEALOUS WHEN SHE DOES. SHE MISSES HER MOM. SHE'S ON THE ROAD SO MUCH SHE HAS TO TAKE 3 GRADE 10 COURSES OVER AGAIN. SHE SAID SHE WAS LONE-LY.

BUT SHE'S **FAMOUS**! SHE MUST HAVE A **MILLION** FRIENDS. HOW CAN SOMEBODY FAMOUS BE LONELY?

...SHE'S TALKING ABOUT THE **PERSON** INSIDE THE PERFORMER.

BECKY WAS ACTUALLY NICE TO ME FOR A CHANGE.

MAYBE SHE LIKED YOUR SINGING!

WHO KNOWS.

ANYWAY...SHE SAID HOW LUCKY I WAS **NOT** TO BE FAMOUS, TO HAVE A REGULAR LIFE AND A REGULAR HOME AND PARENTS WHO WERE STILL MARRIED TO EACH OTHER.

SHE SAID IF SHE COULD TRADE LIVES WITH ME, SHE WOULD.

SO, ... WOULD YOU TRADE LIVES WITH **HER**?

NO WAY!

FOR ONE THING, SHE HAS TO WEAR THESE WILD, AMAZING COSTUMES NIGHT AFTER NIGHT AFTER NIGHT!

WHAT'S WRONG WITH THAT?

...THEY'RE NOT WASHABLE.

WE'RE HOME!...WELL...IT'S THE **NEW** HOME.

THAT'S OK. I'M STARTING TO ACCEPT IT.

BESIDES, COMPARED TO SOME KIDS, I'VE GOT IT PRETTY GOOD. I HAVE A ROOF OVER MY HEAD, A BED TO SLEEP IN AND 2 SQUARES EVERY DAY.

THAT'S **3** SQUARES: BREAKFAST, LUNCH AND DINNER!

NOPE...I MEAN **2** SQUARES!

WHUMP!

I GUESS I DO HAVE A GOOD LIFE. I HAVE A GOOD FAMILY. I'M NOT TOO DUMB AND I'M NOT TOO UGLY.

I'M GOOD AT MUSIC, AND I'M GOOD AT MATH. I THINK I KNOW WHAT I WANT TO DO WITH MY LIFE....AND IF I WORK HARD— I'LL GET THERE.

I HAVE COOL FRIENDS ...NOT TOO MANY ENEMIES. MY TEACHERS LIKE ME. I KNOW HOW TO COOK AN' HOW TO LOOK AFTER MYSELF.

I GUESS I HAVE NOTHING TO COMPLAIN ABOUT!

BUT......I'LL FIND STUFF.

HI, APRIL GUESS WHAT! THE TELETHON MADE 45 THOUSAN BUCKS!! IT'S ALL FOR KIDS WITH SPECIAL NEDS.

TICK TAP TICK TICK TAP

THANK YOU FOR SINGING. YOU AND EVA WERE REALLY GOOD. I'M GLAD BECKY IS NICE TO YOU AGAIN.

TICK-ITTA TAPP TAP TICK

I STAYED FOR ALL THE 24 HOURS. IT WAS VERY COOL. MR. MAYS WHO OWN THE BIG CAR COMPANY ASK ME TO HELP WITH THE TELETHON NEXT YEAR AND GUESS WHAT I SAID YES!!

TICKITA TAP TICK

NOW WHY? CAUSE YOU HELP ME HAVE SELF CONFIDENCE. I AM DIFFERENT FOR A REASON AND I AM GOING TO MAKE A DIFFERENCE.

TICK TAP TIC

LOVE, SHANNON.
P.S. IF YOU EVER NED A FIEND, PLS LET ME NOW.

For Better or For Worse
By Lynn Johnston

CLICK
CLICK
CLICK
CLICK....

HMMM.... THAT'S STRANGE.

CLICK!

MICHAEL, THE WASHING MACHINE WON'T WORK..... AND WE JUST **BOUGHT** IT!!

HMMM...

I'M GONNA CALL THE GUY WHO SOLD IT TO US!

SNORT!!! NO ANSWER. IT'S SUNDAY. THE PLACE IS PROBABLY CLOSED.

YESSS! ... HERE'S A FAX NUMBER. I'LL SEND HIM A MESSAGE.

GRUMBLE, SNORT, FUME...

HUMMMSHHHHH

DEANNA! I FORGOT TO PLUG IN THE WASHING MACHINE! —IT'S OK!!!

IF IT AIN'T BROKE... DON'T FAX IT!

DADDY? CAN I PLAY ON THE SWINGS? SURE! WE'LL BE RIGHT HERE.

FRANÇOISE IS A BEAUTY, ANTHONY.

I THINK SO. ...SHE HAS THE BEST OF THÉRÈSE AND ME.

THANKS FOR COMING TO THE PARK WITH US THIS MORNING.

THANKS FOR ASKING ME.

WE'RE BEING VERY POLITE TO ONE AN-OTHER, AREN'T WE!

I THINK... AFTER SEEING EACH OTHER AT THE WEDDING....

....WE'RE BEING CAREFUL.

PEOPLE CAME LOOKING FOR US AFTER THE WEDDING, BUT WE HID IN THE ROSÉ GARDEN GIGGLING LIKE KIDS.

IT WAS A PERFECT NIGHT... A CLEAR STARRY SKY, BOTH OF US IN EVENING CLOTHES. — IT WAS ALL SO ROMANTIC.

ANTHONY, WHAT TIME IS IT?

THAT'S THE SECOND TIME YOU'VE ASKED ME. — DO YOU WANT THE NIGHT TO BE OVER?

NO...

I DON'T WANT IT TO END!

WHY DID YOU SHAVE OFF YOUR MUSTACHE?

MY DAUGHTER ASKED ME TO.

HER MOTHER SAID IT MADE ME LOOK PROFESSIONAL. ...FRANCIE SAID IT MADE ME LOOK OLD.

NOW, EVERY TIME I SEE MY FACE IN THE MIRROR, IT SEEMS TO BE MISSING SOMETHING!

IT IS!

THIS!

AFTER ALL THESE YEARS, ELIZABETH. AFTER ALL THESE YEARS!

I KNOW.

I SHOULD HAVE ASKED YOU TO MARRY ME WHEN WE WERE BOTH IN UNIVERSITY.

I WASN'T READY THEN, ANTHONY.

ARE YOU READY NOW?

TO GET MARRIED? PERHAPS....HOW ABOUT YOU? DO YOU WANT TO GET MARRIED AGAIN?

SOMEDAY. BUT.... I'M NOT IN A RUSH. I CAN WAIT.

...AFTER ALL THIS TIME.

DADDY, DADDY! CAN I HAVE AN ICE CREAM?

NOT NOW. WE HAVEN'T HAD LUNCH YET. HOW ABOUT AFTER LUNCH?

I WANT SOME **NOW!** PLEASE, DADDY?

PLEASE, PLEASE, PLEASE, PLEASE,

PLEEASE ?

WHY DON'T WE HAVE LUNCH AND SAVE SPACE FOR A GIANT FUDGE AND CARAMEL SUNDAE?!!

OK!

SORRY, ANTHONY... I SHOULDN'T USURP YOUR PARENTING!

WHAT DOES "USURP" MEAN?!

THAT'S THE SOUND 3 PEOPLE MAKE WHEN THEY'RE EATING A GIANT FUDGE AND CARAMEL SUNDAE!

CAN I HAVE THE CHERRY ON TOP?

ABSOLUTELY! YOU GO FIRST!

WHOA! THAT WAS FILLING! I'M GLAD WE GOT THREE SPOONS!

I'LL BE RIGHT BACK.

DADDY? IS SHE A GOOD FRIEND?

YES, SHE IS.

LIKE, A REALLY, REALLY, REALLY GOOD FRIEND?

YES, ELIZABETH IS A REALLY, REALLY, REALLY GOOD FRIEND.

THEN...

CAN WE KEEP HER?

SNIFFFFFF...MMMMMMM...
...TUNA NOODLE CASSEROLE
WITH MELTED CHEESE ON
TOP!

WE ALSO HAVE BURGERS
WITH BACON, ON SESAME
BUNS, WITH COLESLAW AND
STRAWBERRY FUDGE SUN-
DAES FOR DESSERT.

YOU CAN'T CALL IT "JUNK
FOOD" IF IT'S MADE
FROM SCRATCH!

HELLO? IRIS, IT'S ME!

COME IN, DEAR.
THE DOOR'S
OPEN!

I BROUGHT YOU A
CASSEROLE.

TUNA NOODLE!
YOUR DAD'S
FAVORITE!

HOW'S HE DOING?

NOT GREAT.
TODAY, HE'S
ACTING LIKE
A LITTLE KID.

DAD?

NO!

AGE TWO?

APPROXIMATELY.

DAD? IRIS SAYS YOU'RE NOT
HAPPY WITH YOUR PROGRESS.

NO!

ARE YOU WALKING MORE
COMFORTABLY AT LEAST?

NO.

CAN I GET YOU
SOME TEA?

NO!

WOULD YOU LIKE TO
GO OUT?

NO!

ARE YOU
HUNGRY?

NO!

JIM'S BEEN LIKE THAT
FOR A WEEK! - WHAT
SHOULD I TELL HIS
DOCTOR?

THAT HE'S
CONSISTENT!

JIM? ELLY BROUGHT YOUR FAVORITE CASSEROLE. I'LL MAKE SOME SALAD, AND WE'LL HAVE A NICE DINNER.

HE DOESN'T SEEM TO LISTEN TO ME. IF HE IS... HE DOESN'T RESPOND.

HE'S BEEN DEPRESSED. MAYBE WE SHOULD ASK ABOUT INCREASING HIS MEDICATION. BUT... HE'S ALREADY TAKING TOO MANY PILLS!

HE TAKES THESE BEFORE BREAKFAST, THOSE AT NOON, THESE AT DINNER, AND THESE BEFORE BED!

HE'S SO FULL OF CHEMICALS, I CALL HIS STOMACH A HAZARDOUS WAIST SITE!

BOXCAR! BOXCAR! YES!

HE'S READY FOR A NAP, DEAR... I'LL BE RIGHT BACK.

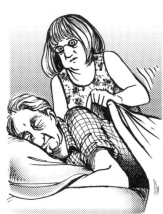

IRIS! YOU'RE CRYING!

NO, DEAR. I.... JUST HAVE A BIT OF A COLD.

YOU ARE CRYING!

LET'S JUST SAY ... IF THE EYES ARE THE WINDOWS TO THE SOUL..... I'M WASHING THE WINDOWS.

HOW'S YOUR DAD?

NO CHANGE. HE'S VERY BAD-TEMPERED — WHICH IS SO HARD ON IRIS.

GROWING OLD ISN'T EASY, ELLY. ANYONE WHO'S OVER 80 AND DOESN'T COMPLAIN HAS MY SINCERE ADMIRATION.

DAD HAS SUFFERED SO MUCH. HE'S LUCKY TO HAVE SUCH A DEDICATED PARTNER.

I WONDER WHICH ONE OF US WILL BE TAKING CARE OF THE OTHER.

I DON'T KNOW, BUT WE COULD START PRACTICING NOW.

YOU HAVE NO SHAME.

... NOT WHEN IT COMES TO BACK RUBS!

SO, YOU AND ANTHONY ARE A COUPLE AGAIN!

WE'RE GOING SLOWLY, CANDACE. IT'S STILL "FRIENDSHIP," OK?

REALLY!—ARE YOU READY TO TAKE ON THE RESPONSIBILITY OF A CHILD, LIZ? WHAT IF THE EX-WIFE SHOWS UP AND CAUSES PROBLEMS?

WHAT IF ANGELIC LITTLE FRANCIE PULLS THE "YOU CAN'T BOSS **ME** AROUND—YOU'RE NOT MY MOM!" THING?

SHE WILL...

—AND I'LL HANDLE IT!... I CAN ALSO HANDLE HER MOM! THÉRÈSE THREW AWAY A WONDERFUL MAN AND A BEAUTIFUL DAUGHTER!—SHE JUST.....THREW THEM AWAY!!!

AND YOU'RE INTO RE-CYCLING!

CANDACE, WHY ARE YOU BEING SO NEGATIVE?

I'M JUST PLAYING THE DEVIL'S ADVOCATE, OK? I WANT YOU TO SEE BOTH SIDES OF THIS RELATIONSHIP!

YOU HAD THE CHANCE TO BE WITH ANTHONY BEFORE, BUT YOU DIDN'T TAKE IT. WHAT'S DIFFERENT ABOUT HIM NOW?

I'M THE ONE WHO'S DIFFERENT.

SNIFF

NON DIP

I GREW UP! AND IN ORDER TO DO THAT, I HAD TO GET AWAY FROM EVERYTHING AND EVERYONE I KNEW. I WANTED TO FIND OUT WHO I WAS.

AND?

ONION

I FOUND OUT WHO I **AM**!

I DON'T UNDERSTAND WHY ANTHONY MARRIED THÉRÈSE IN THE FIRST PLACE.

HE WAS CRAZY ABOUT HER!

DIP

THEY MET AT A DANCE CLUB IN UNIVERSITY. THEY ARE BOTH WONDERFUL DANCERS. THEY EVEN ENTERED A FEW COMPETITIONS TOGETHER.

SHE'S ELEGANT AND SOPHISTICATED. SHE SINGS AND PLAYS THE PIANO. SHE'S OUTGOING AND FUN TO BE WITH.—SHE JUST CAPTIVATED HIM!

SO... WHAT HAPPENED?

I GUESS "CAPTIVATED" BECAME "CAPTURED"!

DIP

MY BROTHER KEPT ME INFORMED ABOUT ANTHONY. EVEN THOUGH WE'D STOPPED SEEING EACH OTHER, WE WERE STILL FRIENDS!

ANTHONY AND THÉRÈSE WERE HAPPY FOR A WHILE... BUT SHE WANTED TO CHANGE HIM.

HE LOOKS LIKE A FOOL TODAY.

SHE CRITICIZED THE WAY HE DRESSED, THE WAY HE ATE AND MADE HIM GROW A MUSTACHE, SO HE WOULDN'T LOOK LIKE A KID!

HONEY, YOU SHOULD CUT THAT IN HALF!!

BUT... YOU CAN'T CHANGE PEOPLE!

NO KIDDING!

EVERY TIME MY MOM TRIED TO CHANGE ME, I GOT ANOTHER PIERCING— THEN I GOT A TATTOO!

I WAS INTENSE BACK THEN, LIZ.

I KNOW. ...AND YOU HAVEN'T CHANGED!

ANTHONY BOUGHT GORDON'S HOUSE AND FIXED IT UP. EVEN THOUGH HE PLANNED TO SELL IT SOMEDAY, THÉRÈSE WASN'T HAPPY. SHE WANTED TO LIVE IN THE CITY.

WHY DIDN'T THEY WORK ALL THAT OUT BEFORE HAND?

I DON'T KNOW, CANDACE.

HER MOM DESPERATELY WANTED GRANDCHILDREN, AND HER DAD KEPT SAYING THAT A HOUSE WAS A GOOD INVESTMENT. BEING AN ONLY CHILD, I THINK SHE DID MANY THINGS FOR THEIR SAKE.

SO, THERE YOU GO AGAIN.... YOU CAN'T CHANGE PEOPLE. YOU HAVE TO TAKE THEM AS THEY ARE.

AND EVENTUALLY THÉRÈSE TOOK ANTHONY FOR ALL SHE COULD GET!

SO, WHY DID SHE HAVE A BABY?

THEY'D BOUGHT A HOUSE. ...I GUESS SHE THOUGHT SHE COULD BUY INTO THE WHOLE DOMESTIC PACKAGE!

ANTHONY WAS THRILLED WHEN FRANÇOISE WAS BORN, BUT THÉRÈSE BECAME DEPRESSED. SHE WENT BACK TO WORK AND LEFT HIM WITH THE BABY.

SHE SPENT MORE AND MORE TIME AT WORK. EVENTUALLY SHE ADMITTED SHE WAS HAVING AN AFFAIR WITH A CO-WORKER. SHE ASKED FOR A DIVORCE, AND HE AGREED.

SHE LEFT HIM WITH THE HOUSE, THE BABY AND A LOT OF DEBT. ...HE'S ONLY JUST STARTING TO TRUST AGAIN.

AND.... HE TRUSTS YOU?

TRUST ME. ...HE DOES.

I HAD AN AWESOME TIME ON THE FARM, DAD. I'VE GOT SO MUCH TO TELL EVERYBODY!

I'M, LIKE, TOTALLY AT HOME WITH THE HORSES NOW. I CAN RIDE ALMOST AS WELL AS LAURA, AND UNCLE DANNY LET ME DRIVE THE TRACTOR **AND** THE TRUCK!

WE WENT TO THE HARVEST FAIR, AN AUCTION AN'A COUNTRY MUSIC FESTIVAL!

WHAT ABOUT THE VETERINARY CLINIC? DID YOU ENJOY WORKING THERE?

OH, YEAH!

THAT WAS THE BEST PART OF ALL! I GOT TO HELP OUT WITH THE SURGERY AN'I SAW STUFF YOU WOULD **NOT** IMAGINE! LIKE, GUTS AN' EVERYTHING!

BUT I'LL TELL YOU ALL ABOUT THAT AT SUPPER.

WELCOME HOME, HONEY!

HI, MOM! 'SNIFF'...WHOA! WHAT SMELLS SO GOOD?!

MEATLOAF.

AND BUTTER TARTS!! YOU BOUGHT BUTTER TARTS!!!

HOW COME YOU GOT THE KIND WITH NO RAISINS?

I KNOW YOU DON'T LIKE RAISINS.

BUT, YOU **LOVE** THEM! HOW CAN YOU BUY BUTTER TARTS WITH NO RAISINS?!

CALL IT A SNACRIFICE.

TWO MORE YEARS, JOHN...AND APRIL WILL BE ON HER OWN.

I KNOW.

I WONDER WHAT IT WILL BE LIKE, TO BE EMPTY-NESTERS.

WE'LL NEVER BE **COMPLETE** EMPTY-NESTERS, EL....

HEY, MOM...WE JUST RAN OUT OF MILK. CAN I BORROW SOME?

GOT ANY MORE BUTTER TARTS?

I SMELL MEATLOAF!

WE'VE ALWAYS HAD AN OPEN-DOOR POLICY... AND AS LONG AS THE FRIDGE IS STOCKED —THEY'LL BE OPENING THE DOOR!